Sarah
1964–

Frances
1979–

George
Earl of St Andrews
1962–

Helen
1964–

Nicholas
1970–

Antony
Armstrong-Jones
1st Earl of Snowdon
1930–
(div.)

= Lucy Lindsay-Hogg
1942–

Edward =
Duke of
Kent
1935–

Katharine
Worsley
1933–

Alexander
Earl of Ulster
1974–

Lady
Davina Windsor
1977

Lord
Frederick Windsor
1977–

James
1964–

Marina
1966–

Richard =
Duke of
Gloucester
1944–

Birgitte
van Deurs
1946–

William
1941–72

Alexandra = Angus Ogilvy
1936–   1928–

Michael = Marie-Christine
1942–   1945–

Henry
Duke of
Gloucester
1900–1974

= Alice Montagu-
Douglas-Scott
1901–

George
Duke of Kent
1902–42

= Marina
Princess of
Greece
1906–68

John
1905–19

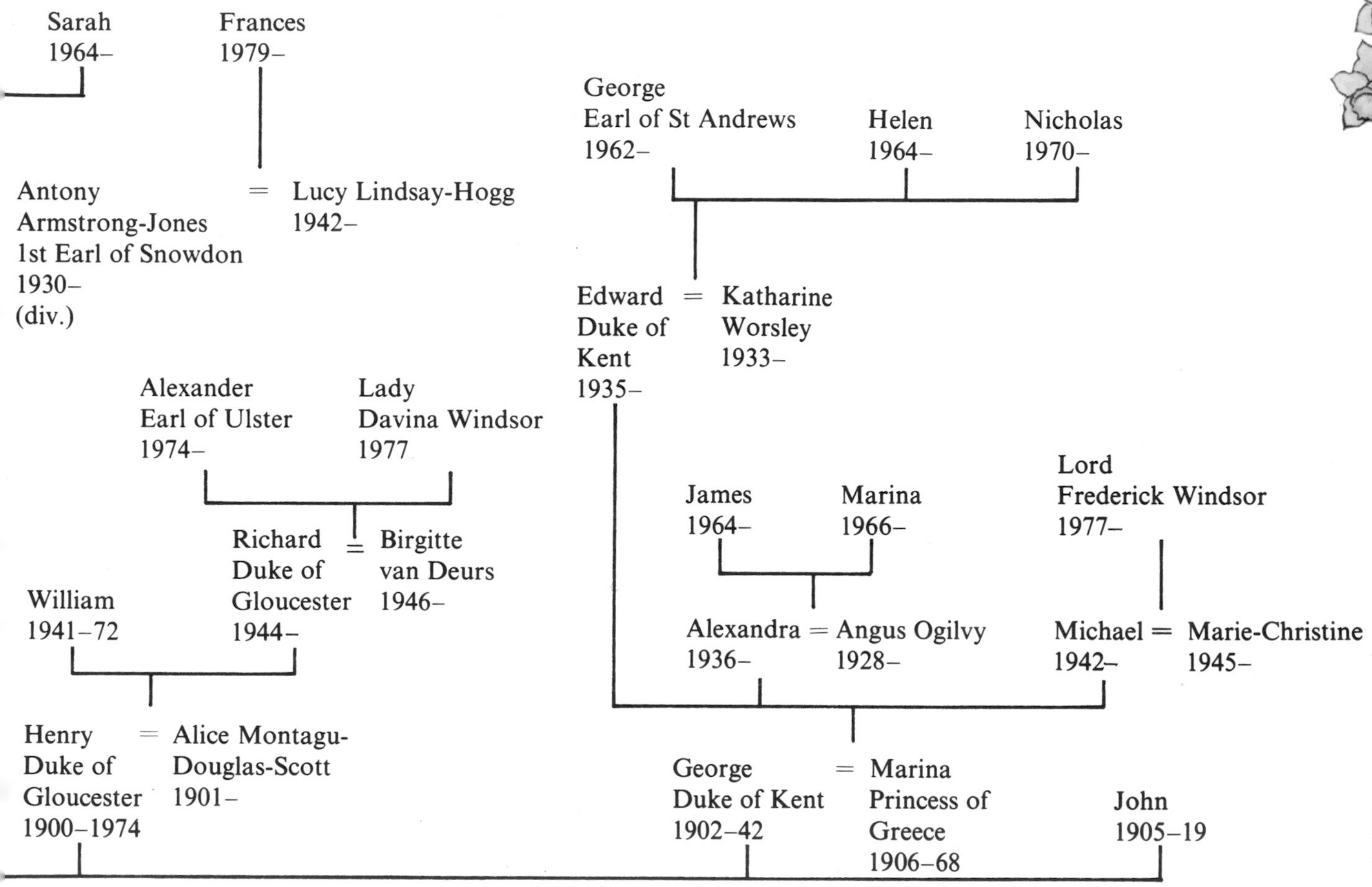

The Royal House of Windsor

George V's proclamation of July 1917
declared that all descendants of Queen
Victoria in the male line would henceforth
bear the surname 'Windsor'. This super-
ceded the title 'Saxe-Coburg-Gotha',
introduced into the British royal family
by Albert, Prince Consort.

This family tree shows the relationship of
all the major figures in *Royal Romance*.

ROYAL ROMANCE

An Illustrated History of the Royal Love Affairs

Crescent Books · Marshall Cavendish

New York · London & Sydney

Editorial team: Linda Doeser Renny Harrop Eden Phillips Felicity Smart Robin Wood
Designer: Annie Tomlin   **Picture research:** Mark Dartford Moira McIlroy

First edition
published and distributed by:

Marshall Cavendish Books Limited
58 Old Compton Street
London W1V 5PA
England

Crescent Books
A division of Crown Publishers, Inc.
One Park Avenue
New York, New York 10016

IN THE U.K., COMMONWEALTH AND REST
OF THE WORLD, EXCEPT NORTH AMERICA

IN THE UNITED STATES OF AMERICA

ISBN 0 85685 836 6 (UK)

ISBN 0-517-29875-9 (US)

Library of Congress Cataloging in Publication Data
Picknett, Lynn
  Royal Romance
  Includes index.
  1. Great Britain — Kings and rulers — Biography.
2. Great Britain — Princes and princesses —
Biography. 3. Windsor, House of. I. Title.
  DA28.1.P52   941.082'092'2 [B]   79-21584 ISBN 0-517-29875-9 (US)

Some of this material was first published
by Marshall Cavendish Limited in
The Royal Papers

First printing 1980

Below: Reception at St Paul's Cathedral before King George V's Jubilee Service 1935, by Frank Salisbury.

Overleaf: The Duke and Duchess of York, later King George VI and Queen Elizabeth, on their honeymoon.

Introduction

When King Canute sat on the beach and commanded the waves to go back, he was demonstrating that even kings have no power over the tides. Nor is a crown any protection against another equally great and relentless natural force—love.

The lives of Britain's Kings and Queens, Princes and Dukes are so different from our own that, to us, royalty itself is romance. Glamorous and exciting, surrounded by the formalities of protocol, the royal family play out much of their lives on the public stage, applauded and cheered, finely dressed and bejewelled.

It is almost a relief to know that royalty are susceptible to the pangs of Cupid's darts. Falling in love is a deeply private event, a brief secret between two people, concealed perhaps from even their closest friends and relations. These are the special moments captured in *Royal Romance*—the times when the man or woman comes first and the King or Queen, Prince or Princess, takes second place.

A lover cannot keep his secret long and a royal lover has less opportunity than most. Once the news of a royal romance is out, the happy couple can rarely escape the glare of publicity and the interested crowds that gather wherever they go. Symbol of the nation itself, the royal family is never surprised that the choice of a husband or wife should be such a public concern. *Royal Romance* celebrates the most memorable occasions—the joyful moment when a couple shyly first holds hands in public; the solemn mystery of the marriage service; the pomp and splendour of state occasions; the delights of parenthood and family life, and the enduring magic of royalty itself.

Contents

KING EDWARD HEARTILY BIDS YOU WELCOME TO HIS CORONATION DINNER, ON JULY 5TH. 1902.

King Edward V11
&
Queen Alexandra

Edward and Alexandra

Prince Albert Edward, Prince of Wales, was only seventeen when his parents began the search for a suitable wife for him. The qualifications for the future Princess of Wales were demanding—she had to be royal, Protestant, of high moral principles, strong enough to bear children . . . and pretty enough to keep her husband's interest. Most importantly, she had to be approved by his mother and father, Queen Victoria and Prince Albert.

Victoria gave more than her name to an era. She had become a symbol of respectability, diligence, duty and the virtues of family life. She was devoted to her husband, Prince Albert of Saxe-Coburg-Gotha, whom she married in 1840.

Their first son, Prince Albert Edward, Duke of Cornwall and the Heir Apparent to the throne, was born on 9 November 1841. Named after his father, he was always known to his family as Bertie. The fact that he had a pet name might be taken as a sign that his childhood was a happy one, full of affection, but that was not so. His grave and conscientious father personally supervised his upbringing and education, and he expected his son to keep to his own strict standards of conduct. This was not in the young Prince's nature and throughout his boyhood he was conscious of being a disappointment to the parents whom he longed to please.

When they came to consider the subject of Bertie's marriage, Victoria and Albert enlisted the help of his elder sister, Victoria, who had made a most satisfactory match in 1858 with the Crown Prince of Prussia. Princess Victoria (Vicky to her family) began searching for a suitable wife for her brother—someone who would guard him against immorality and give him a sense of responsibility. Ideally she would be German, but the list of likely candidates from the royal houses of Europe proved to be surprisingly short. As Vicky herself put it, 'Princesses do not spring up like mushrooms out of the earth or grow upon trees.'

Even the ladies who could be considered had drawbacks: Princess Anna of Hesse had a gruff voice; Marie of the Netherlands was not strong; Princess Elizabeth of Wied was vulgar; Marie Hohenzollern was quite lovely but a Roman Catholic. The only possible choice seemed to be the sixteen-year-old Princess Alexandra Caroline Marie Charlotte Louise Julie of Schleswig-Holstein-Sonderburg-Glucksburg, daughter of Prince Christian of Denmark.

Previous page After decades of Court mourning, the nation rejoiced when fun-loving Bertie became King.

Until he was declared heir to the Danish throne, Prince Christian had been an army officer, with a limited income. Princess 'Alix' and her brothers and sisters had a happy, informal and secure childhood and remained close throughout their lives. Vicky wrote to her mother in praise of the Danish princess, but concluded,

'I have seen several people who have seen her of late—and who give such accounts of her beauty, her charm, her amiability, her frank natural manner and many excellent qualities. I thought it right to tell you this in Bertie's interest, though as a Prussian I cannot wish Bertie should ever marry her.'

The Queen shared her daughter's doubts. She wrote,

'The beauty of Denmark is much against our wishes. What a pity she is who she is.'

Queen Victoria did not want to offend the Prussians, who, for years, had been intent upon making Schleswig-Holstein part of Germany, not Denmark. She also strongly disapproved of the Danish Court, regarding it as lax, chaotic and unroyal.

At this time the Tsar of Russia was also vetting the Princesses of Europe for a suitable wife. After the difficulties she had already encountered in her search on her brother's behalf, Princess 'Vicky' was anxious not to lose the only possible candidate. She made further investigations and was able to put her mother's mind at rest concerning Alexandra's morals, manners, character and family. A meeting was arranged between the Prince of Wales and the Princess selected by his mother and sister to be his bride. Encouraged by her brother's attitude to Alexandra, in September 1861 Princess Victoria arranged an interview with Prince Christian to discuss the match. Everone was well pleased with the arrangement. Even the stern Prince Consort remarked, on seeing a picture of 'Alicky', 'From that photograph I would marry her at once.' The Prince of Wales seems to have had no opinion about his future bride, apart from finding her very beautiful.

The family rejoicing was short-lived. In November 1861, the Prince Consort received information about his son which shocked him deeply. The Prince of Wales had gone to Trinity College, Cambridge, at the beginning of 1861, but he longed to join the Army and, in the summer of 1861, he was allowed to serve with the Grenadier Guards at the Curragh, a training camp

near Dublin. An attractive young actress, Nellie Clifden, well-known to the soldiers before the Prince arrived, was smuggled into the camp one night and found herself in the Prince's quarters. By the time she left them, he had begun the career as a 'collector' of attractive women for which he later became so famous. The story might have ended there had not gossip about

Queen Victoria and her heir. Albert Edward was created Prince of Wales when just one month old. He had to wait 59 years before ascending the throne.

it reached the Court. The Queen and—more importantly—the Prince Consort, were horrified. Already unwell, Albert travelled to Cambridge to confront his son, who begged his forgiveness. Afterwards, quite unhinged with grief at what he called Bertie's 'fall', Prince Albert began to suffer from depression, sleeplessness and loss of vitality. He caught a 'chill', which was eventually diagnosed as typhoid, and, on 14 December, 1861, he died.

Queen Victoria was beside herself with grief. There was no doubt in her mind that the son who had been nothing but a disappointment to his father in life was the direct cause of his death. Writing to Vicky, she said,

'The affair at Curragh was what made beloved Papa so ill—for there must be no illusion about that—it was so; he was so struck down—and I can never see B.—without a shudder! Oh! that bitterness! Oh! that cross!'

And later, in another letter,

'The agony and misery of this day last year when beloved Papa first heard of Bertie's misfortune! Oh that face, that heavenly face of woe and sorrow which was so dreadful to witness! Let Bertie not forget it!'

In the months following her husband's death, Victoria became determined that the only way of saving Bertie was to marry him to Alexandra as soon as possible. In the autumn of 1862 she briefly interrupted a journey to Albert's old home in Coburg, to meet the future bride in Belgium. She assured herself of the suitability of her future daughter-in-law and, having bestowed her approval, made sure that Alexandra was made aware, in a general way, of Bertie's 'failings'. On 9 September 1862, Bertie took Alix for a walk and, with his Uncle Leopold, the King of Belgium, hovering discreetly in the background, he proposed. Alix accepted and that night Bertie wrote to his mother,

'I told her how very sorry I was that she could never know dear Papa . . . I only feared I was not worthy of her . . . I cannot tell you how happy I feel . . . Love and cherish her you may be sure I will to the end of my life.'

The British public, who had never shared the Queen's passion for all things German, welcomed the lovely Princess warmly. Arrangements for the wedding did not go smoothly, however. Churchmen disapproved

of it taking place in Lent but the Queen, reminding them that she was the Head of the Church of England, insisted the service be held on 10 March 1863 in St George's Chapel, Windsor. It was Victoria's intention to keep the ceremony as quiet as possible: the humorous magazine *Punch* suggested that the wedding announcement in the London newspaper *The Times* should be a bald, 'On the 10th inst. by Dr Longley, Albert Edward England KG to Alexandra Denmark. No cards.' The Queen, who had rarely been seen in public since the Prince Consort's death, watched the ceremony from Catherine of Aragon's Closet, a grilled balcony above the nave. She was, of course, dressed in black, but Alexandra wore a white crinoline.

In spite of Victoria's insistence on a private ceremony, there was a procession through the streets of London, before the bridal procession to Windsor, when a huge crowd watched coach after coach carrying members of European royal families pass by. Despite a freezing cold wind, the fact that people were crushed in the press of the crowds and the disgraceful condition of the horses and carriages, Princess Alix's charm won all hearts, including her bridegroom's.

To be the Princess of Wales and the object of praise was a delightful experience for the shy, unspoiled Alix. Her married life began with an idyllic honeymoon at Osborne on the Isle of Wight. Bertie, too, still hurt by his mother's accusation that he was to blame for his father's death, enjoyed his new role as a married man. Alix was beautiful, intelligent, full of fun and not only a wife, but a lively companion. This made a strong bond between them and a fortunate one, for very soon after their honeymoon, the Prince's eye began to rove once again.

In the next six years, Alexandra bore five children; Albert Victor ('Eddy'), George (later to become King George V), Louise, Victoria and Maud. A sixth child, Alexander, lived for only one day. Like most Victorian women of her status. Alexandra had been taught to accept her duty as a wife and to endure sexual intercourse as the means to producing a large family. Bertie, however, liked women, whatever their rank, to enjoy the physical act of making love. This aspect of his nature was apparent to his wife and his mother. *'I often think her lot is not an easy one,'* Victoria wrote, *'but she is very fond of Bertie, though not blind.'*

The birth of the first baby, two months' premature,

Alex and Bertie on their wedding day. The lovely young Danish Princess won the hearts of the British people, and, for a time, of her dashing husband.

may have been hastened by a period of great worry and distress for the Princess. Prussian territorial claims over the Duchies of Schleswig and Holstein, which constituted about half the Danish kingdom, ultimately resulted in open conflict. Alix's intense family feeling was outraged and she was in terror for the lives of her relatives in Denmark. Queen Victoria, absolutely pro-Prussian, saw all her forebodings concerning her daughter-in-law's nationality being fully justified. In the midst of all this trouble, the baby Prince, weighing less than two kilograms (four pounds) was born unexpectedly and had to be delivered into a flannel petticoat.

Prince George, too, was born prematurely, in June 1865, and the Princess became seriously ill with rheumatic fever in the weeks following. She eventually recovered her health but remained lame in one leg for the rest of her life.

Throughout their life together, Bertie regularly gave his wife expensive gifts but less and less of his time. His first real show of heartlessness—or, at least, thoughtlessness—came when Alix was most vulnerable. In February 1867, she was approaching the birth of her third child. Naturally anxious after the difficulties of her previous two confinements, she was especially distressed when this one became both painful and a cause for serious medical concern. The Prince, newly returned from a trip to St Petersburg in Russia, ignored three telegrams urging him to his wife's side and went steeplechasing at Windsor, as he had previously planned. When Princess Louise was born, Alix was delivered without the aid of chloroform and suffering dreadfully both from the pains of childbirth and from the legacy of rheumatic fever which afflicted her hips and leg. She was wretchedly ill and in pain for some months after this, but refused sleeping draughts so that she might wait up for Bertie and have a few words with him, even if it were sometimes three or four in the morning before he returned home.

However, life with Alix had its difficulties for her husband. One of his unswerving qualities was his punctuality; Alix, on the other hand, was almost always late, sometimes by hours. He pretended resignation to hide genuine panic and servants recalled how he would half shut his eyes and huff and puff in disbelief when his beautiful wife limped into the room, asking pleasantly if she were late.

Alix was a 'High' Anglican in her religious observance and her private rooms were a clutter of crucifixes and devotional works. Her prayers occupied three hours each day, a period which Queen Victoria regarded as excessive: in Britain, in her view, religious zeal was measured by that of the Head of the Church—Victoria herself.

For Bertie, the most irritating of Alix's characteristics was that she had maddeningly little idea about the upbringing of children—a matter which by turns bored and terrified her husband. As a child he had feared his own father, who rarely spoke to him but instead wrote him memoranda. He had been educated by a succession of elderly and often unsuitable tutors, and deprived of company of his own age for fear of moral contamination. Perhaps because of his own experiences, he was content to let his wife deal with their children in her own way. Unfortunately, this seemed to consist of indulging them as if they were small children, even when they were grown up, and letting them do just what they liked most of the time. To the end of her life, George called her 'Motherdear' and she often addressed him as 'Georgie Dear'. Queen Victoria found the wildness of the Wales's children most irritating and much preferred the better mannered and more docile grandchildren who frequently visited her from Germany.

After the 'reign' of the Prince Consort 'Albert the Good', London—and the country generally—needed a little gaiety. The Queen shut herself away in seclusion, but the people who were invited to the Wales's London home, the 'Marlborough House Set', began to set a new, faster pace for Society. The horse races once again became the 'sport of kings'—and of those who emulated the Prince; the theatre, opera and ballet were once more patronized by royalty. Members of the aristocracy sought out the best chefs and attempted to out-do each other in entertaining their most appreciative royal guest at banquets and house parties. Not since the reign of Charles II, two hundred years earlier, had Society been so open. Bertie loved fascinating company and, in search of it, crossed the barriers of class and prejudice without causing a stir. Jews, Catholics and commoners found themselves seated next to aristocrats and statesmen at the Prince's table and, to please him, they had to get on with each other.

Alexandra was determined to share as much as a wife and mother could in the life of the Marlborough House Set. Because of her genuine charm and dignity,

Bertie and Alexandra enjoying the sea air. They were familiar figures at the yachting events held at the fashionable resort of Cowes, Isle of Wight.

14

few of her husband's friends or enemies had cause to pity the Princess of Wales. She was more than a match for the glossiest Society beauty, with her regal bearing, her infectious smile and her ability to turn defects into social advantages. She overcame her increasing deafness by treating any speaker whom she couldn't hear to a dazzling smile. Her slight limp was imitated by ladies of fashion and the jewelled chokers she wore to conceal a small scar on her neck set a fashion, too.

The Prince of Wales had a far-reaching effect on Society, even though his pleasure in it skipped a generation in his own family, and emerged again in his lively and popular namesake, Edward VIII. Open and highly cosmopolitan as it was, it was never permissive in the modern sense. Appearances had to be maintained and scandal avoided at all costs: the commandment of the day was 'Thou shall not be found out.'

Despite the efforts of his parents, Bertie had inherited a weakness for the 'fair sex' from his Hanoverian ancestors. Almost any pretty girl could become one of his passing fancies, but it took more than a sparkling eye and a neat ankle for a woman to become one of Bertie's mistresses. They had to be amusing, witty or strong-minded, and some of them were all three. Several remarkable women, including Lady Warwick and Lillie Langtry, were among the Prince's lovers. Different as they were in many ways, they all shared one qualification—they were married. It was an unwritten rule that the Prince's ladies must be married even if it meant that he had to take a hand in finding suitable husbands for them. Married women would be discreet and, should they conceive, there was no need for the Prince to be embarrassed.

Scandal, however, was not always easily avoided and Bertie was a central figure in three major, unsavoury cases. Only two of these involved women. In 1869 Lady Mordaunt admitted to her husband that she had committed adultery and confessed that the Prince was among her lovers. For some time there was a possibility that he would be named as co-respondent in the subsequent divorce proceedings and he escaped public scandal by only the skin of his teeth. He did, however, appear as a witness and denied that there was anything improper in his relationship with Lady Mordaunt. In 1890, the Prince was one of a country house party at Tranby Croft, when a guest was

Bertie pursued his own private version of the 'entente cordiale' with Sarah Bernhardt, the French actress who conquered the hearts of thousands.

accused of cheating at cards, and although there was no suggestion that Bertie had been involved, there was considerable public outcry. Scarcely had the royal family weathered this storm, than he was again involved in the disreputable Beresford case and all the embarrassing revelations of a sordid marital dispute.

Generally, however, Bertie conducted his affairs with discretion, or at least with style. Lillie Langtry, the 'Jersey Lily', famous in Society for her beauty, was his first publicly acknowledged mistress, seen on his arm at the races, balls and the theatre. When she decided to take up the theatrical life herself, no one was more enthusiastic than her royal patron. He personally bought all the tickets for an opening night when the critics threatened to be hostile and he and Alix were always there to congratulate her after the performance. Her association with the Prince lasted for many years. During it, he continued his pursuit of other lovely women, but remained good friends with Lily. He even introduced her to his two sons while they were all sailing at Cowes, off the Isle of Wight—George V remembered the meeting fondly when reading through 'the Jersey Lily's' letters after his father's death in 1910.

Perhaps the most extraordinary aspect of Bertie's complicated social life was Alix's attitude to his

Bertie was a popular figure in Society and the leader of his own 'set'. His colourful personality contrasted sharply with that of his sombre, disapproving mother.

Lillie Langtry as Cleopatra. The 'Jersey Lily', actress and Society beauty, was Bertie's first publicly acknowledged mistress and a long-time close friend.

women friends. Quite early in her marriage, she recognized that her husband was an incurable philanderer and wisely decided that her best course of action was to remain dignified and aloof. She refused to let public outrage at the time of Lady Mordaunt's divorce affect her behaviour and made a point of being seen with Bertie. She was never quite the understanding angel that some have depicted her to be. There were occasions when his behaviour upset her so much that she went away to stay with relatives and at least once she deliberately missed his birthday party. Nevertheless, she took some trouble to get to know personally the women close to him and, indeed, showed some of them extraordinary kindness.

She quickly accepted Mrs Langtry, for example, and no one was heartier in recommending her beauty and her plays than the Princess of Wales. When she discovered that Lillie was going to have a child, she quietly discussed with her what they should do about the baby who could, under no circumstances, be Mr Langtry's: he had been estranged from his wife for years. At the time, when Alix had no way of knowing whether the child was her husband's, her sincere sympathy and lack of censure drew tears from Lillie. (In fact, the Prince was not the baby's father.)

Alexandra was generous to a fault. Her idea of charitable help was large sums of money, given instantly. Certainly she had no idea of the value of money and her unostentatious upbringing in Denmark had not prepared her for budgeting. She had grown heartily sick of sewing her own clothes as a child, and marrying the heir to an Empire was a blessed release from counting the cost of things. If she added to Bertie's wild extravagance, it was, she argued, all in a good cause. It was typical that her first reaction to the announcement of Queen Victoria's Diamond Jubilee in 1897 was to write a large cheque to provide a celebration dinner for London's poor.

Four years after the Jubilee, Queen Victoria died. It seemed symbolic that the Prince of Wales should become King Edward VII at the start of a new century. True, he was fifty-nine, fat and wheezed from incessant

Although partially blind and completely deaf, the widowed Queen, with her still flawless complexion, remained a striking figure even in old age.

cigar smoking, but he was well loved by the people who had almost forgotten the 'widow of Windsor'. His coronation, planned for 28 June 1902, had to be postponed because he fell ill with peritonitis and nearly died. The ceremony actually took place on 9 August 1902. Edward proved to be a wise and talented king, entirely devoted to his country's interests. Throughout her reign, Queen Victoria had consistently refused to give him any real work to do, considering him to be totally irresponsible. She would have been surprised by Bertie's diligence and by his considerable grasp of international affairs.

Time was running out for the high-living King. Rich food, wine and spirits and the innumerable cigars finally took their toll. A chill caught in his favourite city, Paris, in 1910, aggravated his chronic bronchitis. On 2 May he was wracked by a fit of coughing and urged to go to bed. Once there, he

muttered 'Of what use is it to be alive if one cannot work?' He soon began to suffer from great weakness and pain and Alix hurried to him from a holiday on Corfu in the Mediterranean. On 6 May she took a characteristic but quite unprecedented step and sent for the King's last woman friend, the charming and sympathetic Mrs Alice Keppel, so that she could sit with the family beside the dying King. In a lucid moment he said, 'I shall not give in', but, on 7 May, he drifted quietly into what seemed like a deep sleep. 'I have seldom or never seen a quieter passing of the river,' wrote one of Edward's attendants.

The king's body lay in the same room for more than a week before his widow and elder son could be persuaded to set a date for the State funeral. Alex greeted mourners with a tender smile—Lord Esher wrote of her,

'In a way she seemed, and is, I am convinced, happy. It is the womanly happiness of complete possession of the man who was the love of her youth, and—as I fervently believe— all her life . . . Round the room were all the things just as he had last used them, with his hats hanging on the pegs as he loved them to do.'

The funeral took place on 20 May: at Alix's insistence, the King's horse, Kildare, and his dog, Caesar, followed the coffin.

The widowed Queen lived at Sandringham House in Norfolk, her favourite country seat, until she died of a heart attack in November 1925. She spent much of her time playing with any children who happened to be about. Although partially blind, completely deaf and much given to talking to herself, she still enjoyed reminiscences and jokes. She also kept her interest in international affairs and in her international family, although she was saddened by a number of losses: one brother, the King of Denmark, died; another, the King of Greece, was assassinated; and in 1918, her nephew, Tsar Nicholas II, and his family were massacred by the Bolsheviks.

Towards the end of her life her mind wandered increasingly but she drew great comfort from her son, George V, and his family. In one of her last letters to him she wrote, 'You and my darling May are in my thoughts all day long, and all your children.'

Her other comfort was the justifiable belief, held firmly until her death, that of all the women he had cared for, Bertie had *'loved her most'*.

King George V
&
Queen Mary

On 3 May 1893, His Royal Highness Prince George, Duke of York, proposed marriage to his dead brother's fiancee. This was not a love-match, and such an arrangement would be unthinkable to many people today. But 'arranged' it was, as it had been for his brother Eddy, by his grandmother, Queen Victoria. In the royal Court of the late nineteenth century, there was no question of letting private inclinations over-rule public duty.

The marriage may have had the most unromantic of origins, but in the years to come, a deep and abiding love developed between George and his bride, Princess May of Teck, which gave him strength and support through the many national troubles and traumas that were to characterize his reign as King George V.

The second son of the Prince of Wales (later King Edward VII), George was born on 3 June 1865. His elder brother, Albert Victor—like his father, named after Queen Victoria's late husband in deference to her wishes, but known to his family as 'Eddy'—was a year older. George was followed by three sisters, and a brother who tragically lived only for a few hours.

Alexandra, the Princess of Wales, was a devoted mother, called by her children 'Motherdear'. Often deprived of the company and companionship of her husband, she became a possessive, indulgent and affectionate mother. Although the boys, especially Eddy as second in line to the throne, were subjected to very much the same demanding educational schedule that their father had himself endured, their boisterous natures shone through.

As Eddy grew up he proved more and more un-suitable for his future role as the next Prince of Wales. George showed himself to be brighter and more diligent at his lessons when they were children and had more aptitude and self-discipline when they were sent away for naval training. Finally, in order that Eddy should have a chance to develop without being out-shone by his brother at every step, he was sent into the Army and to university, while George remained in the Navy. Eddy was not attractive in appearance: his neck and wrists were so long that his father nicknamed him 'Collar and Cuffs'. A cause of great anxiety was his increasing tendency as he grew up to enjoy the low life of London. He may well have inherited his father's robust and somewhat dissolute tastes, but he did not inherit his charm and good nature. Speculation and stories about Prince Eddy have abounded: it has been said that he frequented London brothels, that he was a homosexual, even that he was the notorious murderer 'Jack the Ripper', who was never caught. Such speculation about the Prince remains no more than speculation, but what is certainly true is that his conduct scandalized the royal family—so much so that it was thought advisable to get him away from England, and he was sent on a tour of the Far East.

Queen Victoria herself was disturbed by reports about her grandson. Although the marriage to Princess Alexandra had only been partially successful in curbing the Prince of Wales's taste for high living, the Queen felt that his son needed the same remedy. For some time Eddy had shown considerable interest in his cousin, Princess Alexandra of Darmstadt, but she refused his offers of marriage and later married Tsar Nicholas II of Russia. Shortly after this, he fell in love with Princess Hélène of Orleans but her Catholicism made her unacceptable as a future Queen of Britain. Eddy then turned his attention to Lady Sybil St Clair-Erskine, but before this had much chance to develop, Queen Victoria intervened. Her suggestion of a marriage between Eddy and Princess May of Teck had all the weight of a royal command. Eddy dutifully proposed on 3 December 1891 and May, equally dutifully, accepted.

Princess May's mother, Mary Adelaide, was the daughter of the Duke of Cambridge, younger brother of Queen Victoria's own father, the Duke of Kent. She had married Prince Franz of Teck, the child of a marriage between Duke Alexander of Wurttemberg and a Hungarian countess, Claudine Rhedey. (The marriage was a morganatic one: Prince Franz's mother was not given a higher rank and he was not entitled to succeed to his father's title or estates.) Later created Duke of Teck, Prince Franz was a career soldier but the early years of his marriage were spent in England at Kensington Palace in London and White Lodge, Richmond. Their first child, Victoria Mary Augusta Louise Olga Pauline Claudine Agnes, was born at Kensington Palace on 26 May 1867; in spite of this catalogue of names, the Princess was known to her family throughout her life as May. During the next seven years, three brothers were born and the children grew very close.

As well as being connected with the British royal family, and through it with many other European royal families, the Tecks were related to the Danish royal house and to a number of German princelings and dukes. May and the other Teck children grew up in a cosmopolitan world with wide social contacts;

Previous page George and Mary in their Coronation robes.

Queen Victoria selected Princess May as a wife for her dissolute grandson, Albert Victor Duke of Clarence, and the couple became engaged in December 1891.

because of her grandparents' morganatic marriage — Queen Victoria considered herself above petty squabbles over rank and settled on May as the ideal wife for the future King of Great Britain and Ireland, Emperor of India and the Dominions beyond the Seas.

She proved a popular choice and crowds cheered her after the engagement was announced in December 1891. Princess Alexandra was delighted and warmly welcomed her future daughter-in-law into the family. The Prince of Wales was charmed by her and Eddy himself managed to be attentive and well-behaved. Victoria, of course, was well pleased, but all the rejoicing was short-lived. In the following January, Eddy developed pneumonia after an attack of influenza (his illness may have been complicated by a venereal infection), and on 14 January 1892, he died.

Although there had never been any suggestion that the young couple were in love with each other, Princess May was deeply distressed and shaken. Her family, too, was acutely disappointed and immediately began making plans for a match between their daughter and the Wales's second son, George. Similar thoughts were stirring in the mind of the Queen. Aware that George would prove a far more suitable and trustworthy heir to the throne than his brother, she saw no reason to change her choice of future Queen consort. George had real affection for May and admired both her character and her gracious good looks. During the next few months they wrote fond, although by no means romantic, letters to one another. When George proposed, May accepted. She had been brought up to believe that the position of Queen was the highest to which she could aspire and she accepted without question the responsibilities she was called upon to fulfill.

among their playmates were the Wales's children. Cushioned for some time against the realities of life, the Tecks received a sudden shock when they realized that their income did not match their rank. The Duke had long since given up the Army when, in 1883, he barely escaped bankruptcy amid public scandal.

The Tecks' debts made it impossible for them to maintain their way of life in England and for the following two years they lived abroad, mainly in Florence. It was here that May began to develop her life-long love for the fine arts and antiques. During this period, from the ages of sixteen to eighteen, May acquired a grace and style which became uniquely her own. When she 'came out' as a debutante at Queen Victoria's Court in March 1886, she won the Queen's approval for her quiet, stately bearing and good manners. From then, May had a constant place in royal society. Although she was an unacceptable match for any of the German princes of the day —

George and Mary, as Princess May became known once she was Queen consort, were married on 6 July 1893, at the Chapel Royal, St James's Palace, London. Some months after their wedding, her husband now the Duke of York, wrote,

'I saw in you the person I was capable of loving most deeply, if you only returned that love . . . I have tried to understand you and know you, and with the happy result that I know now that I do love you, darling girl, with all my heart, and am simply devoted to you. I adore you, sweet May, I can't say more than this.'

May suffered acutely from shyness and George,

basically a highly emotional man, found it hard to express what he felt passionately. They wrote touchingly frank letters to each other but seemed unable to break down the barriers of Victorian reserve when face to face. It was this inability to express their true feelings, except in the written word, that provoked May to this touching reply to one of her husband's letters, 'What a pity it is that you cannot *tell* me what you write, for I should appreciate it so enormously.'

The first of the six York children—'The Regiment', as George called them—the future King Edward VIII, was born eleven months after the wedding. Five others followed; Albert ('Bertie'), the future King George VI in 1895, Mary in 1897, Henry in 1900, George in 1902 and John in 1905. (John suffered from epilepsy and was brought up in the country until he died, in 1919.)

Like many other Victorian women, Princess Mary looked upon child-bearing as a distasteful duty. Unlike her mother-in-law, Princess Alexandra, she was not a devoted and possessive mother. She put her husband's interests and needs before those of her children and her remote, unbending attitude, coupled with her shyness, set her at a distance from her family. She did, however, allow all her children much greater freedom than any previous generation of royal children. George, a delighted and proud father when each of 'The Regiment' was a baby, found growing children almost impossible to cope with. He had been brought up in fear of his own father and saw no reason to change this tradition. His bluff naval humour embarrassed the children and his hot temper terrified them. All of them developed nervous disorders which, in some cases, afflicted them for life.

Queen Victoria consistently refused to delegate any power to the Prince of Wales, even when he had reached middle-age, and so it was not surprising that her grandson had no responsibilities beyond representing her at family weddings and unexciting provincial functions. After his life in the Navy, George chafed at his inactivity and welcomed the opportunity to participate in the Diamond Jubilee celebrations of 1897. In that year, he and Princess May visited Ireland where, in spite of anti-English feeling, they were a tremendous success. Nevertheless, Queen Victoria refused to countenance suggestions that they should become her permanent representatives in Dublin.

On 22 January 1901, Queen Victoria died and the

In July 1893, the handsome, young Duke of York, now second in line to the throne, married his 'shy May'.

Prince of Wales became King Edward VII. He was fifty-nine when he came to the throne and knew that his reign was unlikely to be a long one. Anxious that his son should be better prepared for his future than he had been, he encouraged George to undertake numerous new duties and responsibilities, such as the opening of the first Australian Commonwealth Parliament in Melbourne. He did not bestow the title 'Prince of Wales' until November 1901, feeling that, as he had held the title for so long himself, it might cause confusion in the public mind for George to hold it immediately after him.

Nine years after ascending the throne, Edward VII died. On becoming King in May 1910, George wrote in his diary, 'God will help me in my great responsibilities, and darling May will be my comfort as she has always been.' The coronation of the new King and Queen came after a scandal threatened poor, blameless George. Edward Mylius, a journalist, 'revealed' that George had gone through a form of marriage with one of the daughters of Admiral Culme-Seymour, while on a naval tour of Malta in 1890. The fact that the Prince had not been near Malta in that year and that he had met only one of the Admiral's daughters (when she was eight years old) scotched the story and earned Mylius a year's imprisonment for libel. (There was also talk that George's sudden rages and high colour were caused by drink, but he was, in fact, very abstemious. He was unable to answer these accusations in public but there were times when the noise of his outbursts about them in private made Queen Mary order that doors and windows be closed.)

Coronation Day came and went without a breath of scandal or a mishap. George wrote in his diary, 'The Service in the Abbey was most beautiful but it was a terrible ordeal.' Characteristically prosaic, he finished the entry for that momentous day, 'Wrote & read. Rather tired. Bed at 11.45.'

George came to the throne in the midst of a constitutional crisis. The House of Lords, with a majority of Tory peers, had unprecedentedly rejected the Liberal Government's budget. For the first time in English history two General Elections were held in the same year and the matter was finally resolved, when the Lords agreed to a reformation of their House. This upheaval was a sign of the social and political changes and of the crises which would occur in the next twenty-five years.

However, George's reign was not filled only with problems and worries. He and Queen Mary attended a Coronation Durbar in Dehli in 1911, the first reigning British sovereign and his consort to visit India. The occasion was splendid but, although the King and Queen appreciated the pomp and elegance of the processions, they were also keenly aware of the hungry, restless look on faces in the crowds. In many ways the most conservative of men, the King deplored the fact that educated Indians were refused admittance to the smart Anglo-Indian clubs.

In 1914 World War I broke out—a war which was to change the face of Europe and irrevocably alter society, manners and morals in Britain. On 4 August, the King and Queen stood on the balcony of Buckingham Palace and acknowledged the cheers of thousands. They were to the country a symbol of stability, confidence and essential 'Britishness'. From 1914 to 1918, the King and Queen came into closer contact with the people of their nation than any previous sovereign could have imagined possible and they involved themselves in the war in a way that was new for the royal family. They were photographed 'digging for victory'; they gave up alcohol to set an example; they went to see and comfort the sick and wounded; and they visited and encouraged the troops. As always, duty was a major consideration. The Queen was squeamish and very worried that she would be overcome with pity or grief on the many hospital visits which she felt obliged to make but which she hated. Yet she and her daughter, Princess Mary, the Princess Royal, chatted cheerfully to the dreadfully wounded men without giving any hint of their inner horror and distress—such was their royal training.

The King himself became a war casualty on a visit to France in 1915. The cheering from the men frightened his horse and it fell, rolling on him, breaking his pelvis in two places and causing internal injuries from which he never fully recovered. He also suffered deep emotional and psychological wounds. Many of his own relations and those of his wife were German and the Kaiser was his first cousin, the son of Queen Victoria's eldest and best-loved daughter, Vicky. So many of the kings and princess involved in the terrible conflict had been his playmates in childhood. 1918 brought the crushing blow of the massacre of Tsar Nicholas II and most of his family.

In spite of their German ancestry, the King and Queen had no doubts about where their loyalties lay, but the British people grew more and more antagonistic towards anything or anyone remotely connected with Germany. Germans who had become British citizens had their windows broken and went in fear for their lives. Many people objected to the names of members of the royal family—Saxe-Coburg-Gotha, Teck and Battenberg, for example. George found this hysterical reaction to mere names ludicrous but he finally agreed that the names should be changed by Royal Proclamation. On 17 July 1917, the Battenbergs took the name Mountbatten, the Tecks became Cambridges and, after much research, the house of hyphenated Teutonism became the House of Windsor.

The year 1918 saw not only the fall of the Romanov dynasty in Russia, but also the end of many other European royal houses. Defeat in Europe brought the overthrow of the German Kaiser and the Austrian Emperor and the downfall of many dukes and princes. But 1918 also brought a badly needed peace. Once again, the King and Queen stood on the balcony of Buckingham Palace to acknowledge the cheers of the crowds.

The years following the war were not easy ones, with widespread social unrest and increased trouble in Ireland. Paradoxically, it was George who tried to make life smooth for Britain's first Labour Government. When he received Ramsay MacDonald, the first Socialist Prime Minister, in 1924, the King deliberately wore a red tie and dispensed with the tradition of full court dress. Both men came out of the meeting surprised at the strength of their respect for one another.

Both the King and Queen were essentially traditionalists and placed a Victorian value on duty and hard work. Nevertheless, they also had a remarkable capacity to yield gracefully to change. And change there certainly was, through the gradual transfer of power to the middle classes, the rising political consciousness of the working class, universal franchise and the far-reaching effects of the world economic crisis of 1929 to 1931.

George and Mary remained as popular as ever, but, with the coming into being of the House of Windsor, came the beginnings of a new, more approachable and human monarchy. True, they did not go on walk-abouts, but the King did speak to the nation on the wireless during the war—and when he delivered his regular Christmas message.

On 6 May 1935, King George V celebrated his Silver Jubilee in true royal style and London rejoiced. When he saw the affection and pleasure felt by so many people, he said, with great surprise and a touching modesty, 'Do you know, I really think they like me for myself.'

Within a year he was dead. An abscess on the lung

Increasingly eccentric in old age, Queen Mary still remained a forceful influence in the royal family.

They never took a meal alone, but always with an equerry present, and usually in silence. They had separate bedrooms throughout their married life. And yet the King once broke down with emotion in mid-speech trying to say the words, 'When I think of all I owe her.' For Mary, the husband she loved was also the King she honoured and she never, even in marriage, set aside the awe she accorded the Crown.

Queen Mary's widowhood began anxiously when Edward VIII abdicated, and ended with the joy of seeing a well-prepared and dutiful young Queen about to follow in the footsteps of her father and grandfather. Mary was never idle, nor one to give way to self-pity, although she was capable of sympathy and of great compassion. It was she who rallied the grief-stricken Duchess of Kent after her husband's fatal flying accident; it was she who kept in touch with the son who had, in her eyes, betrayed his royal trust by abdicating, and, in contrast, it was she who indulged her grand-daughter, Margaret Rose, as she had never spoiled her own children.

Throughout World War II, she set a stern example. She observed the rationing regulations scrupulously (never eating even one extra egg), and she ordered a line to be painted on the baths in her households to show the level of water. Her only comment about Hitler was that 'he speaks such abominable German'.

She seemed increasingly eccentric in the modern world, with her pearl 'chokers', her high, rippling coiffure, her long skirts and whaleboned figure. Because she apparently never smiled, this made her all the more remote, but the truth was that she was too shy to smile because she believed that she looked like a horse when she did. Her one attempt to wear skirts a modest two or three inches shorter in the 1920s met with a rebuff from her royal husband. So, set firmly in the Edwardian mould, she personified the old virtues to a forbidding extent.

She lived to play with her great-grandchildren, Charles and Anne, and then, as if willing it, died quietly just before Queen Elizabeth's coronation, on 24 March 1953, leaving express instructions that there was to be 'no fuss'. Hers had been an extraordinarily full life, spanning the reigns of six monarchs, encompassing two world wars and witnessing staggering social, economic and technical change. In a letter to her son George shortly before his wedding, Victoria had written, 'I am sure she will be a good, devoted and useful wife to you': Mary's whole life proved how right that judgement was.

and bronchitis with complications gradually weakened him. He was also deeply worried. The times were unsettled, and when he saw so many royal houses toppling, George felt deeply concerned for the future of the British monarchy. He was particularly anxious about the Prince of Wales's passion for Mrs Simpson which was daily becoming more of a scandal. 'After I'm gone, the boy will ruin himself in twelve months,' he said to his wife. She is reputed to have voiced the opinion that it would be far better if a miracle should happen and the throne were to pass to Bertie and Elizabeth, and through them to their daughter, Elizabeth. The dying King could only agree. King George the well-beloved, as he came to be known, slipped into his last sleep, rousing himself for a moment to enquire about the welfare of the Empire. 'It's absolutely all right, Sir,' may well have been the last words he ever heard. 'Darling May' kissed her husband for the last time and turned to her son, the new King, Edward VIII.

By modern standards, even royal ones, the marriage of George and Mary had been a strangely formal one.

King Edward VIII
&
Wallis Simpson

An ominous and prophetic note was sounded from Edward's very birth in 1894. In the House of Commons, Keir Hardie, the great Socialist leader, spoke against a motion to present the King and Queen with a 'humble address' of congratulations because he thought that the birth was not worthy of attention from Members of Parliament, the nation's democratically elected rulers. He said,

'From his childhood onward this boy will be surrounded by sycophants and flatterers by the score and will be taught to believe himself as of a superior creation. A line will be drawn between him and the people he is called upon some day to reign over. In due course, following the precedent which has already been set he will be sent on a tour round the world, and probably rumours of a morganatic alliance will follow and the end of it all will be the country will be called upon to pay the bill.'

Keir Hardie's words contained many disquieting truths. Edward, or David as he was known to his family and friends, was brought up to believe himself a special person and possibly this gave him the idea that he could get away with anything. But then, to be born third in line to a throne on which Queen Victoria would still sit for a further seven years of her sixty-three-year reign made him a special person. However, there was more to the formation of his character than this, for David was no less influenced by his family background than are others. A great love certainly existed between his parents but it was of an undemonstrative kind and not the sort which could be shared with children. Queen Mary was so reserved, so rigidly regal that David never had the security of motherly love so vital to a child's emotional development.

Both his parents had been raised under the scrupulous and all-seeing eye of Queen Victoria and their whole lives were dedicated to her standards of royal duty and responsibility. Moreover, George V, as second son, had not been destined to be King. He came to the throne in the midst of a constitutional crisis and his twenty-five-year reign saw more crises and changes than almost any other in recent history. The standards set by these essentially Victorian

parents must have been awesome for all their children, growing up in the rapidly changing world of the twentieth century, but particularly so for David, as heir to the throne.

The young Prince of Wales established a style which became uniquely his own. He battled against custom to be allowed near the trenches in World War I and succeeded. He made a series of foreign tours and was greeted with hysterical adulation everywhere he went. He was the first member of the royal family to speak on the radio and the first to be photographed smoking. He seemed to herald a new age for the royal family and stories of his open, easy-going, democratic manner abounded. He mixed with people from all walks of life, played the banjo and danced in London nightclubs until dawn.

This handsome, lively and, above all, modern young man was truly the world's most eligible bachelor. Within him, perhaps as a result of his emotionally deprived childhood, was a desperate need for a supporting and loving relationship with a mature woman and, for him, this always meant a married woman.

In spring 1918, he met Mrs Freda Dudley Ward during an air raid, and began a relationship that would last sixteen years. Their affair was common knowledge in London Society and they met frequently in semi-public places. Yet no hint of scandal ever appeared in newspapers, an interesting indication of a different morality and a different attitude to the royal family and the upper classes from our own. When Mrs Dudley Ward divorced her husband in 1931, there was no mention of her friendship with the Prince, let alone a suggestion that they were lovers. David telephoned her every day and often sent his car and chauffeur to her daughter Angie's school to encourage her to play truant. In fact, he enjoyed playing at 'father' to both her daughters. She was the ideal paramour for a Prince, causing no upset in royal circles because she thoroughly understood what being a royal mistress meant. Whatever her own feelings, she knew there must be no scandal. Besides this, she was a devoted mother and would never have left her two daughters by running away with anyone. Perhaps it was this attitude which caused his other, minor flirtations during the course of their relationship, and, ultimately, his desertion of her.

The Prince's other notable liaison was with Lady Furness. They travelled on safari together in 1928 and Lady Furness described their passionate association in graphic detail in her memoirs some thirty years later. The Prince's amorous activities caused dissen-

Previous page *King for less than a year, Edward VIII renounced his throne for a life of exile, rather than be forced to abandon the woman he loved.*

Lively, handsome and thoroughly modern, the Prince of Wales seemed assured of a happy and unclouded future.

Wallis in 1928, the year she married Ernest Simpson. Two years later, she met the Prince of Wales.

sion in the royal party and news reached the ears of the King and Queen who had always tried to ignore any aspects of life of which they did not approve. Their expression of disapproval had little effect on their son.

It was through Lady Furness that David met Wallis Simpson in 1930. Until that moment, Wallis's life had been difficult and undistinguished. Born in 1896 into a well-bred American family, the Warfields of Baltimore, she nevertheless knew poverty from early in her life. Her father died only five months after her birth, leaving her mother penniless. Until her mother remarried, they were bailed out financially by her father's brother, Uncle Sol. Her aunt, Bessie Merryman, also helped them, and was later to figure largely in Wallis's life as her companion during the Abdication crisis. Thus, at an early age, Wallis, who hated being a 'poor relation', learnt the power of money and position.

Although not particularly pretty, she was still very attractive to boys because of her bubbling personality and self-reliant nature. Out of these qualities developed the mature woman who was to captivate three

husbands. She had an understandable desire to marry for money, but she was also a passionate woman and the man who in 1916 became her first husband, Lieutenant Earl Winfield Spencer Jr, was anything but rich. An aviator, one of the new heroes of that generation, he fascinated the nineteen-year-old girl who found him immensely attractive. But his career in the US Navy did not prosper and he proved unstable. He took to drink and became jealously possessive of his wife. He also played cruel, practical jokes on her, locking her up alone for hours. Despite strong disapproval from her respectable Warfield relatives, Wallis decided on divorce and this was granted in 1927.

Two years earlier she had met Mr and Mrs Ernest Simpson in New York. The Simpsons' marriage was breaking up and the unhappy husband and Wallis, estranged from her husband, were attracted to each other. Ernest, who was of mixed English and American parentage, was a naturalized British citizen. A good dancer, fond of the theatre and well-read, he was an accomplished and cosmopolitan man. In 1928, he and

Wallis were married and settled down together in London. They were very happy.

Ernest's sister, Mrs Kerr-Smiley, was married to an Englishman and lived in Belgrave Square, the most fashionable part of London. She introduced Wallis to London Society, including Lady Furness, the Prince of Wales's current favourite. In turn, Lady Furness, very unwisely as it happened, introduced Wallis to the Prince. Ironically, it was at Mrs Kerr-Smiley's house that the Prince had also first met Mrs Dudley Ward.

It was by no means love at first sight at that momentous meeting in the autumn of 1930. She was very nervous but pleasantly surprised to find that the Prince of Wales was quite relaxed and much more informal than she had expected. She and the Prince discussed the different attitudes to central heating in Britain and America—hardly a thrilling topic to signal the start of one of the greatest royal romances of all time. But the seed was sown. Six months later, the unfortunate Lady Furness invited Mr and Mrs Simpson to a reception at which the Prince was to be present. Again the conversation was brief and unremarkable. A third and, apparently, equally casual meeting resulted ultimately in an invitation to join a weekend house-party at Fort Belvedere, the Prince's country retreat near Windsor Park, in January 1932. Two more house-parties to which the Simpsons were invited followed later in the year. As always, Lady Furness was present.

By 1933, the Simpsons were frequent guests of the Prince and in June he gave a dinner party at the exclusive Mayfair restaurant, Quaglino's, to celebrate Wallis's birthday. The Simpsons also entertained the Prince at their London home. During Lady Furness's long absence on a trip to America, the friendship ripened and became more informal. Before she left she had lightheartedly said to Wallis, 'I'm afraid the Prince is going to be lonely. Wallis, won't you look after him?' Later, news reached the Prince that Lady Furness had flirted outrageously with Prince Aly Khan and his indignation at this may have driven him into Wallis's arms. Whatever the cause, she now emerged as firm favourite and the Prince dropped his other love, Mrs Dudley Ward, whom he had continued to see until 1934. She was doing much good work on his behalf by setting up the Feathers Clubs, named after his royal insignia, to help the unemployed. He ended their relationship with callous abruptness, by simply giving instructions that none of her telephone calls were to be put through.

She never saw him again.

It was at this time that gossip about the Prince and Mrs Simpson really began. He started to give her presents of fabulous jewellery. Lady Diana Cooper, the celebrated hostess and beauty, described her as 'glittering' and said that she 'dripped in new jewels and clothes'. Some suggested that the enormous stones were fakes, but they were wrong. The Prince himself had always been a leader of fashion, starting the vogue for wearing large, loud 'Prince of Wales checks', to the annoyance of King George V, who saw any departure from convention as a sign of serious moral decline. Now David and Wallis became the 'Beautiful People' of their day. Wallis was deeply excited by the glittering and glamorous world she had entered. She was thrilled by the power which placed the finest hotels, the best restaurants, trains and yachts at their command. She was impressed, too, by the calmness and naturalness of his power.

A blissful Mediterranean cruise on Lord Moyne's yacht was later followed by a skiing holiday and a trip to Vienna and Budapest. During this period, they openly declared their love for each other and David reached the decision that he must make her a permanent part of his life. Did he realize that this decision would ultimately mean a choice between the throne and exile? The evidence is that he did not.

Wallis Simpson, who so enchanted the Prince of Wales, was neither young nor beautiful. She was thirty-eight (he was forty) in 1934, the year when she and David first declared their passion for each other. Lady Furness, her defeated rival, described her in her autobiography:

> 'She did not have the chic she has since cultivated. She was not beautiful; in fact she was not even pretty. But she had a distinct charm and a sharp sense of humour . . . Her eyes, alert and eloquent, were her best feature. She was not as thin as in her later years—not that she could be called fat even then; she was merely less angular. Her hands were large; they did not move gracefully, and I thought she used them too much when she attempted to emphasise a point.'

So David fell for a plain woman with big hands, fine eyes, charm and a sense of humour—or was Lady Furness being just a little catty about the woman to whom she had lost her lover? It seems not. Sir Henry Channon, the distinguished diarist known as 'Chips', first described her as 'a nice, well-bred mouse of a

The Prince of Wales kisses his mother's hand at the Silver Jubilee celebrations of 1935. Just over a year later he was an outcast from country and family.

woman, with large startled eyes and a huge mole'. Later he described her as being sensible, witty and, above all, charming.

The royal family was becoming seriously disconcerted by the affair. Many of the jewels showered on Wallis were family heirlooms and this alone caused disquiet. Previously, the family had treated the relationship as just another of David's flirtations but it soon became apparent that this was serious. The old King died in 1936 and some have claimed that his eldest son's behaviour may have hastened his end. Whether that is so or not, for two years, between 1934 and 1936, neither of his parents could bring themselves to break through their reserve and speak to their son about his personal life. Nor, it seems, did his brothers and sister make any attempt to advise or influence him, although the Duke and Duchess of York showed their anxiety and disapproval courteously.

When King Edward VIII came to the throne he was already known and loved by his people. On his accession it was said,

'King Edward VIII comes to the Throne as no stranger to his peoples. Few, very few, of his subjects can rival the knowledge which his travels have brought him of almost every part of the Empire. Thus it also happens that, at a time when the Crown has come to play a new and predominant part in the political unity of the Empire, its wearer is, thanks to his own indomitable energy and to his father's foresight, known "in his proper person" to an unprecedented number of his subjects. "We saw the Prince" has been the delighted claim of hundreds of thousands of overseas citizens in past years . . . "We know the King" will be their no less proud boast today . . .'

Edward VIII intended to be a new kind of king— one who communicated with his people—not a traditional monarch, like his father, remote and shrouded in mystique. There were those, however, who considered that he was not entirely fitted for kingship. He worked at irregular hours and thought nothing of telephoning his staff at any time of the day or night. Worse still, there were worries about him as a security risk. State papers were frequently returned from Fort Belvedere with marks left by wet wine glasses on them. Stanley Baldwin, the Prime Minister, was so worried by this that he took the unprecedented and unconstitutional step of withholding confidential documents from the boxes sent to the Fort.

The King began his reign with a flurry of energetic activity but soon lost his enthusiasm for the day-to-day grind of office work and many papers were returned, obviously unread. His impulsive way of making controversial political statements annoyed and embarrassed the Government. His inability to recognize the threat of Hitler and Mussolini and a few ill-chosen words in one speech earned him the reputation of being a German sympathizer during the time leading up to World War II.

Resentment of Wallis grew among the royal family and the staff of the royal households. She now acted as the King's hostess, giving orders and receiving guests. But she and the King remained more or less oblivious to all this and she even described herself as 'Wallis in Wonderland' to her husband. Ernest Simpson had been patient, tolerating his wife's royal friendship. He had retired to his study to work during David's visits and frequently went away on business trips to America. By 1936, he had had enough and one night at dinner with the King, he demanded that Wallis should choose between them. The King responded, 'Do you really think that I would be crowned without Wallis by my side?'

In the summer of that year, the new King broke with the royal tradition of visiting the royal residences and he and Mrs Simpson, as she still was, took another cruise. This time, aboard the *Nahlin*, they sailed along the Dalmatian coast. The foreign press followed them everywhere and they certainly made headline news. In Yugoslavia the crowds shouted 'Zivila Ljubav', meaning 'Long live love'. They were photographed together everywhere and the King shocked convention by appearing frequently dressed in nothing more than shorts. Only one incident soured the lovers' mood. During a discussion about the King of Greece's relationship with a married woman, Wallis enquired why they did not marry. The other guests explained that a king could not marry a woman who was both a commoner and already married.

When they returned to England, divorce proceedings were beginning. It was Ernest who provided grounds for divorce by becoming involved with another woman. He may genuinely have sought the comfort of another woman's love when his own marriage was falling apart, but there can be no doubt that this was convenient for his wife and the King. Until this time, the royal family, the Government and the King's advisers, including Walter Monckton, had felt that while Mrs Simpson was married there could be no real danger. Now that a divorce was a possibility, the relationship between David and Wallis approached a constitutional crisis because she, a woman with two living ex-husbands, would be free to marry the King.

While the foreign press revelled in the scandal, every effort was made to keep the British press quiet. Walter Monckton persuaded the press barons, Beaverbrook and Harmsworth, to make a 'gentleman's agreement'. As they owned practically all the major British newspapers between them, this was effective. But nothing could stop the avalanche of letters from British citizens living abroad which arrived daily at the Government offices in Whitehall, denouncing the disgraceful behaviour of the King and Mrs Simpson.

Eventually the Prime Minister was forced to confront the King, requesting that he put a stop to Mrs Simpson's divorce proceedings. The interview achieved nothing. Meanwhile, *The New York Journal*, owned by William Randolph Hearst, trumpeted forth across the Atlantic 'The King will wed Wally.' The divorce hearing took place in the country town of Ipswich, birthplace of Cardinal Thomas Wolsey in the sixteenth century. The British press still kept silent, but in America the headline was 'King's Moll Reno'd in Wolsey's Home Town'.

The question of abdication was first raised by the King at this time, but it is doubtful if he considered it as a serious possibility, rather as a threat, a big stick to shake at the Government. Once the divorce was a reality, the aim of the King's advisers was to get Wallis out of the country, but this did not work out either and, instead, she moved to Fort Belvedere with her aunt, Bessie Merryman. Increasing pressure was put on the King to give her up. Alexander Hardinge, the King's Private Secretary, pointed out that soon the British press would break its silence and the whole matter would come to a head. On 16 Novem-

Amid a torrent of publicity, the King and Mrs Simpson spent the summer of 1936 on an Adriatic cruise. Mrs Rogers (left) was a close and sympathetic friend.

ber 1936 Edward spoke openly to his mother for the first time about his love for Wallis. She was deeply sympathetic and appreciated the strength of his feelings but to her the position of a King was a sacred responsibility and the question of duty came between them. She was shocked to the core by the idea of abdication.

The next day, the King spoke to his brothers and told them that he was prepared to abdicate if that was the only way he could marry Wallis. Predictably, they too were deeply shocked—Bertie, the Duke of York, more than anyone. The Duke of Gloucester was concerned as he would have to act as Regent to his young niece if anything happened to Bertie, and the Duke of Kent's reaction was one of anger and disgust.

But this was not the end of the crisis. Towards the end of the month, Esmond Harmsworth, editor of the *Daily Mail*, suggested to Wallis the possibility of a

morganatic marriage. If this was the only way, the lovers were prepared to try it. Such a marriage would be legal but meant that the King's wife could not become Queen and had no claim on his possessions or those of his family, and no children of the marriage would have any right to succession or claim on the family possessions. Morganatic marriages were not uncommon among the royal houses of Europe, but the only precedent in British history was that of George IV and Mrs Fitzherbert in 1785. Stanley Baldwin consulted his Cabinet and the governments in the Dominions. The answer was a resounding refusal. The King then demanded that Parliament should be consulted. New legislation would be required and this

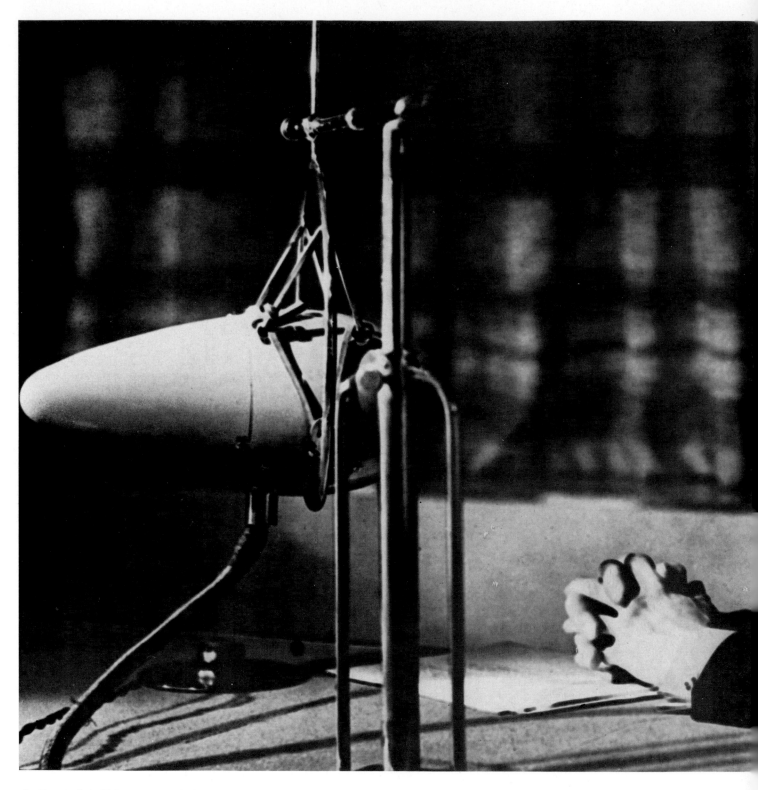

In December 1936, tired and clearly distressed, the uncrowned King made his historic broadcast to the nation revealing his decision to abdicate.

could split the Government. This would mean a General Election with the King's marriage as the decisive issue, an unacceptable situation.

Meanwhile, the British press could keep silent no longer and at last the affair came into the open. The provincial press was largely unfavourable but the national daily papers were sympathetic. The love of a man and woman, in any other circumstances an intensely private concern, became a public controversy. No single event in the twentieth century has caused

conversation.

In the south of France, Wallis was under pressure to make a public renunciation of the King. In fact, she did, but to no avail. Edward was not going to let her give him up. He knew now without a shadow of a doubt that he must abdicate. Any lingering hopes that they could marry and that he could still retain the Crown were shattered. What could be tolerated and even admired in the young and dashing Prince of Wales was unacceptable in a middle-aged King. Perhaps Edward's supreme confidence that Wallis would eventually be accepted had blinded them both. In any case, Wallis, from a different society a world away, could never have fully understood the demands on and attitudes to a traditional British King.

In December 1936, King Edward VIII broadcast to the nation:

> '*You must believe me when I tell you that I have found it impossible to carry the heavy burden of responsibility and to discharge my duties as King as I would wish to do without the help and support of the woman I love.*'

And so, 'Bertie', Duke of York, became George VI and the King became the Duke of Windsor. On 3 June 1937, at the Château de Candé near Tours, Wallis Warfield Simpson became the Duchess of Windsor. Lady Alexandra Metcalfe was present at the wedding and noted in her diary,

> '*She was in a long blue dress, short-fitting tight coat, blue straw hat with feathers and tulle, the loveliest diamond and sapphire bracelet which was his wedding present.*'

Of the Duke, she says,

> '*It could be nothing but pitiable and tragic to see a King of England of only six months ago, an idolized King, married under those circumstances, and yet pathetic as it was, his manner was so simple and dignified and he was so sure of himself in his happiness that it gave something to the sad little service which it is hard to describe. He had tears running down his face when he came into the salon after the ceremony. She also could not have done it better.*'

more debate in homes, pubs, offices and shops. Wallis began to receive abusive and threatening letters. At last, she agreed to go abroad and left for Cannes. The intense nervous strain also began to tell on the King. Winston Churchill, one of his strongest allies, recalled that during a dinner party, Edward went into a daze several times, completely losing the thread of

Behind them, David and Wallis left a legacy of bitterness. The shy, highly-strung Duke of York had

never been consulted about becoming King and was untrained and ill-prepared. The monarchy was embarrassed and the royal family bewildered. David was naively astonished when it was made clear that he would have no role in public life and bitterly humiliated on his wife's behalf when he learned that she would not have the title 'Royal Highness'. He never forgave this, believing it to be a deliberate insult.

Did they think the world well lost for love? Who can really say? Those who knew them after the abdication said that his love for her amounted almost to an obsession, but others—among them Harold Nicolson—thought differently. Writing in 1955, he thought that the Duke 'pretends to be very busy and happy, but I feel this is false and that he is unoccupied and miserable'.

The years following the abdication were difficult for the Windsors. As war approached, the Duke offered his service to the War Office but was fobbed off with vague promises. A visit to Hitler in 1937 made matters

Above *A visit to Hitler's Germany in 1937 prompted speculation that the Windsors were Nazi sympathisers.*

Left *On 3 June 1937, Wallis and David were privately and quietly married at the Château de Candé in France.*

worse because it seemed to confirm rumours that the Windsors were Nazi sympathisers. In fact, they found the Nazi leaders 'repulsive' and, in any case, David's understanding of politics was limited and naive. In Britain, it was believed that, if Germany won the war, the Duke would be made a puppet leader and there is evidence that Nazi politicians toyed with the idea. Whether the ex-King, soured by his change of fortune from adored Prince to royal outcast, ever seriously contemplated such a possibility is a matter for speculation.

With the fall of France in 1940, it became imperative that the Windsors return to England, where their strange status was a great embarrassment. It was decided, therefore, that they should be sent to one of the outposts of the Empire. The Duke was appointed Governor of the Bahamas and he proved to be energetic, popular and fair-minded. Wallis became President of the Bahamas Red Cross and helped with the 'bundles for Britain' campaign which sent supplies to wartime Britain. She also achieved something of a record by cooking and serving with her own hands 40,000 plates of bacon and eggs in the Armed Services' canteen.

After the war the Windsors returned to live in Europe. They chose France as their home in what has often been called their 'self-imposed exile'. They travelled frequently to the United States and were lionized wherever they went. They became the undisputed leaders of French Society in a country traditionally more tolerant of the dictates of the heart than her more puritanical neighbour across the sea. Their Paris home was a constant reminder to visitors that it belonged to a King, however remote from the throne. Crests and coats of arms abounded, the footmen wore livery and the chef was said to be the best in France.

Did time heal the wounds between the Windsors and the royal family? Sadly, it seems not. In 1945, David saw his mother for the first time in nine years and Queen Mary still refused to receive his wife. It was undoubtedly a daunting interview and a photograph taken at this time shows him looking haggard and plucking nervously at his tie. Seven years later, King George VI died and the Duke returned home to walk beside the coffin of his younger brother alongside the young Duke of Kent, the Duke of Gloucester and the Duke of Edinburgh. He must have been aware of all the eyes on him and the unspoken question—had the strain of kingship, forced upon him by the abdication, caused George VI's untimely death?

Far from fizzling out as many predicted, the reckless romance grew into a mature and enduring love.

On 25 March 1953, he returned to England once more for the funeral of his mother but did not stay for the coronation of his niece, Queen Elizabeth II. He himself had not been crowned. Whether or not he was officially invited to Elizabeth's coronation remains uncertain, but he was quoted as saying that it would not be 'constitutional' for him to be present. He watched the ceremony on television in France and was moved to tears by the almost mystical sincerity with which she made her vows. Despite the royal family's coolness towards him, his admiration for the young Elizabeth never dimmed. She too always felt kindly towards him and from childhood referred to him as her 'favourite uncle'.

As a public figure he never really lost his attraction and popularity in Britain. Whenever he and the Duchess were spotted on their brief visits an enthusiastic crowd would gather and often there were cries of 'Welcome home Teddy'. The newspapers would print headlines such as 'Women wait hours to mob the Duke.'

In 1967, the Queen officially invited the Windsors to attend the unveiling of a memorial to Queen Mary. The ex-King with Wallis by his side was cheered heartily by the crowds, but the Duke's health was breaking down and photographs show him looking old and ill. During a State visit to France in 1972, the Queen visited him, but by then he was so ill that he had to receive her in his upstairs sitting room. Not

long after, he died.

At last, Wallis had the whole world's sympathy as she arrived in London for her husband's funeral in June 1972. Though married to a King, it was the first time she had been to Buckingham Palace as a guest of the monarch. A large crowd gathered to see her arrive. She entered the Palace by the Privy Purse door—the door reserved for ordinary visitors. Inside the Palace a small luncheon party was held for her, but it soon became apparent that the strain was telling. She retired to her apartment overlooking the Mall. Occasionally her grief-stricken face could be seen at the window during the Trooping the Colour ceremony the following day, by coincidence her thirty-fifth wedding anniversary. At the Queen's wish, a tribute to the Duke was included in the ceremony. In the

The Windsors rarely returned to Britain after 1936. For the Duke, 'Home is where the Duchess is'.

evening, Wallis, accompanied by the Prince of Wales and Lord Louis Mountbatten, went to see her husband where he was lying in state at Windsor. The Duke was buried privately in the royal burial ground at Frogmore and space beside him was reserved for the Duchess.

The love story of David and Wallis has become a romantic legend, more poignant than any of the Hollywood fantasies it so often resembled. In many ways the Duke himself was the epitome of this legend.

Although he rarely granted interviews to the press, when asked where he considered 'home' to be, he replied, 'Home is where the Duchess is'.

Prince George of Kent
&
Princess Marina

Prince George, later Duke of Kent, the fourth son of George V and Queen Mary, was born in 1902. Bright, high-spirited, often extremely wilful, Prince George was not afraid of anyone or anything. He was the only one of the six royal children who did not go in fear of his father when the King erupted into one of his furious rages. He was closer to his mother, too, inheriting her love of beautiful things. He was taught French by the same governess who had taught Queen Mary and, unlike many members of the royal family, he spoke the language well. In fact, he went on to learn several other foreign languages and even amazed the Dutch on one occasion by managing to speak some of their own notoriously difficult tongue.

Like most royal sons, he was earmarked for a career in the Navy and duly went first to the Royal Naval College at Osborne and then to Dartmouth. He was appointed to the flagship of the Mediterranean Fleet as midshipman and soon rose in the ranks, gaining certificates in gunnery and navigation. More to his liking was his appointment as French interpreter because, for all his diligence in his naval duties, he was at heart an artist rather than a sailor. Seasickness and poor digestion made life afloat miserable for him.

In fact, poor health put an end to his career at sea. After ten years in the Navy, apart from time spent on three long royal tours, he was invalided out. He was quite ill for some time afterwards although he was too active in temperament to allow himself a long convalescence. In the early 1930s he was appointed an inspector of factories and took the job extremely seriously. He alarmed factory committees of the day with his campaign for a five-day working week, which then seemed a wildly impossible idea.

Far enough removed from the throne to be able to relax without feeling anxious or guilty, Prince George thoroughly enjoyed life. His natural charm and good manners made him a popular companion. He was not fond of 'hunting, shooting and fishing', the pursuits which the men of the royal family were expected to enjoy: his idea of fun was to enter the tango dance contest in Cannes under an assumed name and win it. He adored speed, owned a five-litre Bentley and often borrowed the Prince of Wales's private plane for jaunts on his own or with friends. Like his eldest brother, he was very much of his generation, revelling in the exciting, restless post-war world of the 1920s.

He was also a man of cultivated tastes. What he had heard his mother say about art and antiques when he was a child bore fruit and he began to build up a valuable collection. He loved the ballet and was very well informed about most aspects of theatre. In fact, he seemed destined to become the official Royal Patron of the Arts. His keen artistic appreciation and urbanity even led him to understand the subtleties of female fashions. Many English ladies of that time tended to be either over-dressed or boringly tweedy, but one exceptionally elegant young lady of his acquaintance pleased his discerning eye—Princess Marina of Greece.

At her birth in 1906, a gypsy predicted Marina's future:

> 'This is the child of destiny . . . she will be very beautiful and make a marriage with the son of a king. Love will be her guiding star, but it will bring her sorrow too, for she will lose her husband whilst she is still young and at the height of her happiness but she will find consolation in her children.'

A child of the turbulent Greek-Danish royal houses, Marina was used to sudden reverses of fortune. With almost monotonous regularity Greek kings have been exiled and then suddenly found themselves back in favour and the objects of wild adulation. By descent Marina was connected with almost all the royal houses of Europe, so her upbringing was extremely cosmopolitan. She often visited England—Queen Mary was her godmother—but she was totally unknown to the British public until the announcement of her engagement to the dashing Prince George on 28 August 1934. In fact, she was so unknown that the engagement threw the newspapers of Fleet Street into a panic as they had no photographs of her on file. They had to send to Yugoslavia, where she was staying. When photographs did appear, everyone was astonished at her beauty and chic. Even the imperturbable and old-fashioned King George V was won over by her beauty and charm. Queen Mary, her friend already, thought she might be a settling influence on her son.

The wedding of the newly-created Duke and Duchess of Kent took Britain by storm. No one now can be sure exactly why this was so: Prince George

Right *Unaware of the tragedy ahead, George and Marina were passionately and devotedly in love. Here they pose in the gardens of Buckingham Palace.*

Previous page *Paris, traditionally the city of lovers, welcomes the debonair Duke and his delightful fiancée, Princess Marina, on a visit in 1934.*

was undoubtedly very popular and Princess Marina had won everyone's heart; it was the first royal wedding to be broadcast on the radio; and it was the last public occasion when the members of many royal houses would be seen in their splendour; but none of this entirely explains why Britons went wild as never before or since.

While Marina was being dressed in her shimmering gown of silver lamé brocade and her glittering tiara, her groom slipped out to cash a cheque, saying that it would give him something to do! The Prince of Wales was best man and among the bridesmaids was Princess Elizabeth, the Duke's niece and future Queen. Marina's cousin, Prince Philip of Greece, was one of the guests.

In the grounds of the Kents' much-loved family home, Coppins, the Duchess shares a joke with her son, the Duke, and her elegant daughter, Alexandra.

No matter how many people thronged the streets, cheering themselves hoarse, Marina remained firmly convinced that it was all happening to someone else, and that the enthusiastic reception was for her beloved George and nothing to do with her. Time was to show that her adopted country loved her for herself then and throughout her life.

At first, the Kents lived in London's fashionable Belgravia, but when their first son, Prince Edward, was born in 1935, they moved to Coppins, a house in the Buckinghamshire countryside. They had inherited this peaceful country home from Queen Victoria's last remaining daughter. It was an idyllic time and it does seem that the Kents were that rare thing, the perfect couple. He was handsome, knowledgeable and urbane and she complemented him perfectly with her beauty, charm and polished manners. True, the Duke could sometimes be moody, domineering and impatient. He insisted on organizing the household,

selecting the menus, the wines and the table decorations for the many tremendously successful dinner parties which he and his wife gave. He never lost his interest in the details of fashion and often advised Marina on what to wear. Sometimes he even told his guests who to talk to round the table! The Duchess seemed quite happy not to make decisions and to be completely acquiescent. Husband and wife adored each other and theirs was a blissfully happy marriage.

Later, a member of the royal family said of Marina, 'He was her all; he filled her whole life and her whole existence.' But if her husband was the pivot of Marina's life, she was no less the focal point of his. On a visit to her native land, the Duke once said, 'Greece has given me a wife, the full extent of whose influence over me I shall probably never know.' With the births of two more children, Princess Alexandra in 1936 and Prince Michael in 1942, the Kent family was complete. The delighted parents lavished love and attention on their children: the Duke was reported to spend more time in the nursery than in his study.

His many talents, especially his gift for organizing people with tact and charm, were not fully used and so the King, on the advice of the Government, decided to appoint him Governor General of Australia. This would take the British royal family right into the heart of the Commonwealth and the proposal was received with the greatest enthusiasm by Australian politicians. The Duchess was a little sad about moving so far away from their happy country home and from her numerous European relatives, but she quickly caught her husband's excitement about the project. They spent many hours together poring over maps and studying volumes on everything Australian.

The Duke and Duchess never reached their new country. For some time the threat of war in Europe had been growing and when it became a reality in 1939, there was no further question of any of the royal family leaving the shores of Britain. At home the Kents settled into a happy routine, interrupted by occasional air raids. Whenever it was possible, they spent their time at Coppins, where the Duke 'dug for victory' in his much-loved garden and played with their children. But, like all the royal family, they were not idle during those bleak days. The Duchess assumed the name 'Nurse K' (generally understood to be 'Nurse Kay') and worked in a London hospital. The Duke was seconded to the Royal Air Force, a role he expanded to include numerous rounds of factory inspections, just as in his pre-war duties. He also made a memorable trip to Canada, where he threw away his carefully prepared notes and gave a straight-from-the-heart talk about conditions in wartime Britain. The Duchess was appointed Rear Admiral in the Women's Royal Naval Service. This undoubtedly did a great deal for recruiting women into the Navy in those grim days, even if she sometimes infringed dress regulations and never learned to salute properly.

On 25 August 1942, the Duke set off in a Sunderland flying boat from Scotland on a secret mission to Iceland. Miles off course and in wretched weather, the plane crashed on a mountainside in north Scotland. The forty-year-old Duke was killed instantly.

For Marina this was a shattering blow. She had lost the handsome, debonair husband whom she loved devotedly, she was left with three children, one only seven weeks old, and a very small income. For a time it seemed that she would never recover from her grief. Finally, Queen Mary, setting aside her own motherly sorrow, gently reminded Marina of her duty as a mother to go on with her life. This she did, bravely and gracefully, but she always felt that her husband's death had killed part of herself.

For the next twenty-five years Marina took great pleasure and comfort in bringing up her three children. With characteristic courage, she auctioned off many of the precious antiques so lovingly collected by her husband and taught her children thrift. It made her very happy to see her eldest son Edward, ('Eddie'), the present Duke of Kent, married to the lovely Katharine Worsley in 1961, and she was equally delighted when her popular daughter Alexandra married Angus Ogilvy in 1963. Her children helped to fill her life and she also took on many public functions: her flair for putting people at ease made her much in demand. Her favourite official patronage was connected with tennis, a sport she adored. Her last public appearance was to present the trophies at Wimbledon in 1968.

Just a few days later, on the anniversary of her husband's death, she attended a simple family memorial service. She remarked afterwards that she felt tired and went to bed. She never woke up. Although she must have suffered for some time with the brain tumour which finally killed her, it was typical of her courage and dignity that she never allowed this to interfere with her duties. She remained, to the last, kind, witty and beautifully elegant—everything her husband, the royal family and the British people had always loved and respected.

THE CORONATION OF OUR KING AND QUEEN

6D

A WONDERFUL SOUVENIR OF AN HISTORIC CEREMONY

King George VI
&
Queen Elizabeth

The future King George VI began his life on 14 December 1895, the anniversary of the death of his great-grandfather, the Prince Consort. Prince Albert had died forty-four years earlier but Queen Victoria was still mourning her loss. In his honour, the baby was named Albert and Queen Victoria was asked to be his godmother. She duly sent her great-grandson a bust of the Prince Consort as a christening present.

Albert ('Bertie' always to his family) did not have a happy childhood. A puny and unprepossessing toddler, he was told to hush and kept out of sight. He did not endear himself to Queen Victoria by crying with fright when taken to visit her. To make matters worse, his elder brother, David, later Edward VIII, was everything a prince was expected to be.

By the time his father, George, Duke of York, came to the throne as King George V, the family had increased by four more children, three sons and a daughter. While they were still babies their father enjoyed them and, in fact, often nursed them, boasting 'I make a very good lap'. But as they grew up, he became a remote and frightening figure to them. Even his joviality was overpowering. His own father, King Edward VII, whose aim was to rear relaxed and vivacious children, had only succeeded in frightening them with his growly voice, his massive presence and, worst of all, his over-hearty chaffing. Although George never put happiness above duty for his children, he maintained his father's tradition in one thing—the abrasive teasing.

It was no use running to their mother for comfort. She was an intensely controlled and private person and her shyness extended even into her relationship with her children. Brought up and married in the stern Victorian tradition of royal responsibility and duty, she once said, 'I must always remember that their father is also their King.' Nevertheless, she did spend time with them. She took them on tours of the various royal houses, explaining the history and value of all the paintings, antiques and jewels. Art was Queen Mary's abiding interest, but only her fourth son, George, Duke of Kent, took after her as an eager collector of beautiful things. The others stood too much in awe of their mother to benefit very much from her knowledge.

'Bertie' did, unhappily, inherit his mother's shyness and later in life was to show a sense of duty and aware-

Previous page *Ill-prepared for kingship, George VI found lasting support in the love of his wife.*

The young Duke of York cuts a dashing figure in his Naval uniform in spite of his extreme shyness.

ness of public responsibility as great as hers. Throughout his childhood and adolescence he was overshadowed by his bright and lively elder brother. In his studies, David was erratic but often brilliant. Bertie, finding oral work difficult, being inarticulate, slow to learn and painfully shy, was chided and repressed. Also, despite being naturally left-handed, he was

Surrounded by canine companions, a young Lady Elizabeth relaxes at her family home, Glamis Castle.

made to write 'like his brother' with his right hand. This certainly contributed to, if it did not actually cause, the stammer that was to make speech so hard for him throughout his life.

At Dartmouth Naval College, throughout his time in the Royal Navy in World War I and at Cambridge University, the Prince never shone. He was dogged by ill-health and handicapped by extreme nervousness. At Cambridge, a tutor remarked that the young Prince was 'an ugly duckling to Edward's cock pheasant'.

The unhappy, unfulfilled Prince seemed destined to plod through life in sad obscurity—until he suddenly, and totally unexpectedly, fell in love. He had first met Elizabeth Bowes-Lyon at a children's party when he was nine and she was five. (Many years later he recalled how she had given him the crystallized cherry from her sugar cake.) They met again during the 1920

Season—the time of the year given up to all kinds of social events—at one of the small London parties which his parents felt were suitable for their bachelor sons to attend. Elizabeth danced enchantingly all evening, watched shyly by Bertie from the edge of the dance floor.

It could not be described as a blazing start to the romance, but the lonely Bertie was overwhelmed, to the exclusion of everything else in his life. He was too shy to speak of his love but he made sure that he was invited to the same parties as Elizabeth. She was a friend of his younger sister, Princess Mary, so he had 'inside information' on her movements. He was also, once or twice, a guest at Glamis Castle, Elizabeth's family home.

In due course, a close friend of Bertie's sounded out Elizabeth's feelings on the Prince's behalf and was sharply snubbed. But the go-between was shrewd enough to suspect that this was the response of a spirited girl who would answer differently if approached direct. So Bertie declared his feelings. On Sunday, 13 January 1923, he proposed to Lady Elizabeth in a wood at St Paul's Walden Bury in Hertfordshire, where they were both staying as house guests. She accepted. Two days later, the engagement was formally announced. Thereafter, King George V and Queen Mary treated Elizabeth as their own daughter. They found her charming, pretty and 'different'.

Different she certainly was. She had been brought up with great informality as the youngest daughter in a large, boisterous and talented Scottish family: her father was the fourteenth Earl of Strathmore. Born on 4 August 1900, she was christened Elizabeth Angela Marguerite Bowes-Lyon: the family had Stuart blood on her father's side and her first name came from Elizabeth Plantagenet, daughter of Edward I.

The ninth child in the family, she was doted on from the beginning: she was said to have had a smile in her cornflower-blue eyes from the moment she opened them. Never spoiled, she quickly developed a charm and imperious manner that earned her the nickname 'Princess' Elizabeth long before there was any thought that, one day, a royal title would be hers by right.

Lady Elizabeth's childhood at Glamis Castle in the Scottish glen of Strathmore was idyllic, especially because it was shared with her brother, David. Two years her junior, he was her inseparable companion until he was sent away to school. Left to their own devices, the children would amuse themselves on fine days in the grounds, fishing, making friends with the animals and playing in a secret hideaway. She had a very happy childhood and combined an impish sense of mischief with her tremendous charm. The Strathmore family was a fine mixture of fun and high standards, self-confident without being affected or self-important, and kind and considerate to other people. Their strong sense of family feeling meant that their evenings together, gathered around the piano to sing, playing charades or other parlour games, or simply telling stories, were a source of delight.

Elizabeth was fourteen at the outbreak of World War I. One wing of Glamis Castle was turned into a convalescent home for soldiers and Elizabeth helped her mother with the running of it. Although she could not do nursing, she could brighten the lives of the

The coronation in May 1937 gave many subjects the opportunity to demonstrate the depth of their affection for the new King and his radiant Queen Elizabeth.

wounded. This was when she first discovered that she had a very real talent for putting others at ease and cheering them up. The patients looked forward to her visits and she was scrupulous about sharing her time equally between them. She played cards, wrote letters, played the piano and sang and offered cheerful encouragement. She also indulged the mischievous side of her character by dressing up her brother David

as a lady, with plenty of padding, a large hat and white gloves. She then gravely took him round the hospital beds and introduced him as 'A Very Important Visitor' to all the patients.

When Elizabeth was eighteen she began to take part in London's social life. She renewed her friendship with Princess Mary, whom she had met previously at Glamis. Inevitably she met the Princess's brothers and came under the watchful eye of Queen Mary. The Queen liked the pretty, level-headed, intelligent girl and made a mental note of her

as 'good queen material' and a possible match for the Prince of Wales. But it was Bertie who fell under the spell of Lady Elizabeth's charm. She was a popular girl and received many proposals of marriage from a number of eminently eligible suitors before she finally accepted the young Duke of York.

Her first experience of the press was a pleasant foretaste of things to come. They went into raptures over the Duchess-to-be—and never changed their opinion of her. The nation, too, was delighted. Won over by Bertie's steadfastness, and heartened by the affection of the delighted King and Queen, Lady Elizabeth

Her gown of chiffon mousmé and the bridal veil of Point de Flandres lace, Lady Elizabeth Bowes-Lyon, in the height of fashion, leaves for Westminster Abbey.

reacted with startled pleasure to the flood of congratulatory messages after the announcement of the engagement. Such immediate acceptance and popularity strengthened the sense of duty and responsibility she was to act upon from that time forward with dignity and warmth.

The first public sign of Lady Elizabeth's graceful diplomacy was her choice of bridesmaids. Three were her intimate friends, Diamond Hardinge, Betty Cator and Lady Katherine Hamilton. Three others had royal connections and had been bridesmaids to her friend, Princess Mary. The other two were her own nieces, Cecilia Bowes-Lyon and Mary Elphinstone.

The wedding was on 26 April 1923. It was the first

wedding of a royal prince at Westminster Abbey since that of Richard II in 1383. The bride's gown was of chiffon mousmé, cut in the medieval fashion with a centre panel of silver lace threaded with ribbon, running from the neckline to the hem. Queen Mary presented the bride with a Pont de Flandres lace veil which she wore over her forehead in the 1920s style. At the last moment she forgot her gloves and long afterwards fashionable brides dispensed with them in imitation.

It came as a disappointment to many that plans to broadcast the wedding service were not sanctioned by the clergy of the Abbey, who feared that 'the Service might be received by persons in Public Houses with their hats on.' The royal wedding procession, greeted with tumultuous enthusiasm, was led by the coach carrying the King and Queen, followed by that of the aged Queen Alexandra and her sister, the exiled Empress of All the Russias. Prince Albert was reported as looking 'pale'. At the very moment the bride walked into Westminster Abbey, the sun came out from behind a cloud and sunlight streamed in on those gathered inside in their colourful court robes and uniforms.

From the beginning of the Yorks' life together, magazines and newspapers welcomed opportunities to show photographs of the young Duchess, who was noted for smiling more than any other lady in the royal family. Shortly after Easter in 1926 she gave birth to a daughter, who was christened Elizabeth Alexandra Mary, breaking with Queen Victoria's rule that all children close to the succession should bear her name or that of her beloved Albert. The King and Queen were delighted with the baby and the press celebrated the happy event. The birth had no special significance for the nation, for the Duke of York came after his elder brother, the Prince of Wales, in the line of succession to the throne. Apart from this, it was probable that the Yorks would have more children, and if one of them were a son, he would take precedence in the line of succession.

A second daughter, Margaret Rose, was born in 1930. Their family life was a great joy to the Duke and Duchess. Moreover, the King and Queen were able to enjoy the company of their grandchildren and grow close to them in a way that had never been possible for them with their own children. Throughout the early 1930s the Yorks lived a quiet, peaceful and domestic life. Although he remained a modest man all his life, the Duke gained a new confidence and strength from the love and support given so freely to him by his vivacious and lovely wife. The couple carried out many public engagements and much that they did was characterized by a shared concern for the under-privileged in society, the poor and the unemployed.

In 1936, the Abdication of Edward VIII shook the world and the unprepared and unambitious Bertie suddenly found himself King and the inheritor of a shaky throne. George V, who had died earlier in the same year, had reserved his skilled tuition in matters of state for his eldest son. The Duke of York, who took his father's name as King George VI, had had no chance to equip himself for his totally un-expected role, and it was perhaps the most difficult time in history to take over an empire. Dictators were dominating the political scene in Europe; certain sectors of the British public wanted a republic; others, with right-wing views, called for the return of Edward VIII. In addition, the new king shared in the grief his brother's abdication had caused the whole royal family and was full of anxiety about the responsibilities he would be placing on the shoulders of his elder daughter, who was only ten years old, and next in line of succession.

But the British people saw in the new King and Queen a good man and a devoted wife. Above all, they saw the stability of a loving family established again round the throne. The coronation gave pleasure to millions in darkening times. The King's voice held steady throughout the long ceremony and Elizabeth was every inch a Queen.

As the Duke and Duchess of York, the couple had always worked together and now, in the demanding role of King, George VI was even more sustained by the strength of his wife, as Queen Consort. They embarked upon their public duties wholeheartedly and earned love and respect everywhere they went. In their busy public round they still managed to find time to be with their daughters and took an active part in organizing their education.

Queen Elizabeth made friends everywhere. At the outbreak of war in 1939, she showed an unerring sense of occasion by wearing black velvet at the State Opening of Parliament. No one had ever seen her so beautiful, regal and grave. Equally characteristically, she was one of the first to be fitted with a gas mask. She knew that such simple acts could radiate an influence on the ways in which ordinary people behaved.

Throughout World War II, the royal family stood at the head of a family of nations, united in purpose,

Throughout World War II, the King and Queen, as head of their 'larger' family, remained in London—a symbol and inspiration to a beleaguered nation.

and the reassuring voice of the King was heard, in exactly the right mood, in his first Christmas broadcast after the outbreak of war, when he spoke the familiar words of comfort, 'Put your hand into the Hand of God. . . .' The religious faith of the King and Queen was a source of strength to the people.

During the German bombing raids on London, the King and Queen spent much time in the devastated streets of the capital's East End, comforting and cheering the people. In September 1940, Buckingham Palace was bombed while they were in residence.

Although they were shaken, they felt it was right to have shared the experience with other Londoners. The Queen declared, with typical directness and simplicity, 'I'm glad we've been bombed. Now we can look the East End in the face.' Because of their feeling of responsibility to the nation, which they saw as their own, very large family, they decided against sending their daughters to a place of safety abroad, when other parents were unable to do so.

On VE Day, the day on which Victory in Europe was officially declared, the royal family had to appear again and again on the balcony of Buckingham Palace, where they were joined by the Prime Minister, Winston Churchill. The throngs of people below cheered, danced and sang as the King and Queen looked on. They had all worked together throughout the war years and now it was fitting that everyone should celebrate together.

The war had prevented the King and Queen from devoting as much time to family life as they would have liked. They set about enjoying the pleasures of parenthood with renewed vigour and the first few months of peace were among the happiest of the King's life. Princess Elizabeth was now no longer a child but a young woman with a mind of her own and a young woman in love. Both the King and Queen were anxious that the Princess's attachment to the young Prince Philip of Greece might be the infatuation of a young, inexperienced girl. The King was inclined to be a possessive father but the Queen had a more relaxed view, although she was equally concerned for her daughter's happiness. They decided that the young couple should test their feeling for one another by a period of waiting.

Early in 1947 the royal family toured South Africa. The King had been looking forward to the visit, eager for the chance to unwind and relax with his family, away from the cares of State. He was already beginning to show signs of the illness which would eventually cause his premature death. Two months after the family returned to Britain, the King and Queen acknowledged that their beloved daughter was truly in love and the engagement between Elizabeth and Philip was formally announced. The wedding, which took place in November that year, was a source of great pride to the royal parents and they wished their radiant daughter a happiness as great as their own in her married life. The King wrote to the Princess,

'I have watched you grow up all these years under the skillful direction of Mummy, who as you know is the most marvellous person in the World in my eyes and I can, I know, always count on you, and now Philip, to help us in our work.'

Indeed, the King had to count on his daughter more and more as his health failed. In 1951 he had undergone a major operation and seemed to make a good recovery, but, on the morning of 6 February 1952, when his valet carried the usual cup of tea to his bedroom, he found that the King had died peacefully in the night. The day before, George had been out shooting for six hours at Sandringham, the royal estate in Norfolk. He had spent a typical quiet evening with his wife and Princess Margaret and they had listened to radio news of Princess Elizabeth and her husband on their tour of Africa and Australia. At eleven o'clock he went to bed, read for a while and drank a cup of cocoa. Some time during the night, coronary thrombosis, which had been a constant threat since his operation, ended the King's life.

For thirty of his fifty-six years, George VI had been supported, encouraged and loved by his devoted wife. She had attentively nursed him for more than three years through his illness and had been delighted and hopeful to see an improvement in his health in recent months. At his death she must have sorely missed her elder daughter who, in this moment of cruel loss, became the Queen. The widowed Queen Consort must have been aware, too, that there was to be little time in the immediate future for private sorrow. In death, as in life, she had to share her husband with the nation. But there was only one wreath on the King's coffin, white flowers, bearing a card inscribed, 'Darling Bertie from his always loving Elizabeth'.

A gracious lady and a beloved grandmother, the Queen Mother plays with Prince Andrew in August 1960.

Lord Louis Mountbatten
&
Edwina Ashley

orn in 1900, Louis Battenberg, as he was then called, was part of the charmed circle of European royalty. The son of one of Queen Victoria's granddaughters and Prince Louis of Battenberg, he was connected by birth to almost all the European royal houses still surviving at the beginning of the century. Queen Victoria agreed to be his godmother and the baby Battenberg repaid the honour by knocking her spectacles off her nose. He was christened Louis Francis Albert Victor Nicholas, but was known to his family throughout his life as Dickie.

At the outbreak of World War I, almost everything even remotely connected with Germany was hateful to the British people, in a totally unreasoning way. Anyone with a foreign name ran the risk of being insulted by the normally easy-going British. And what could be more German than Battenberg—except perhaps Saxe-Coburg-Gotha, the King's own family name? This vicious surge of misplaced patriotism drove Prince Louis to resign from the office of First

Previous page The last Viceroy, Lord Louis shared with Edwina a special and lasting affection for India.

Below Dickie (right) and his close friend and cousin, the Prince of Wales, enjoying a bath stretched between the guns of HMS Renown in 1920.

Sea Lord at the Admiralty, less than three months after the declaration of war, in spite of forty-six years of distinguished service with the Royal Navy. His career was virtually ruined and his son, who had been a naval cadet since 1913, also had a hard time. At this point, King George took the family name of Windsor and Queen Mary's family, the House of Teck, changed its name to Cambridge. The Battenbergs anglicized their name by straight translation to Mountbatten. When the Kaiser heard of these changes, he remarked that he was looking forward to seeing the play, *The Merry Wives of Saxe-Coburg-Gotha!*

It was all very well for the Kaiser to scoff, but for his young second cousin in England, it was a serious matter. Louis Mountbatten set out to vindicate the family reputation. The scars were, and remained, very deep. The Naval College, Osborne, Isle of Wight, was a harsh training ground for the young man—all the more so because he was his father's son, the discredited First Sea Lord. But the Navy was his career and he was to emerge as one of the finest leaders and commanders in World War II, serving as chief of Combined Operations, and eventually as Supreme

Right The carefree newly-weds, Dickie and Edwina, wave goodbye as they set off on board the Majestic for their idyllic honeymoon in 1922.

Dickie and Edwina, seen here with their elder daughter in 1937, delighted in parenthood without letting it interfere with their exceptionally busy lives.

Allied Commander in South-East Asia.

In 1920, Louis Mountbatten's parents were visited by Edwina Ashley, daughter of Sir Wilfred Ashley, later Lord Mount Temple. She was a spirited 'flapper', a member of the 'Prince of Wales's set' of lively and sophisticated young people, and extremely beautiful. He was immensely attracted to this lovely, lively and charming girl, heiress to the Cassel banking fortune. When her multi-millionaire grandfather, Sir Ernest Cassel, died, Dickie realized just how great this fortune was and decided that Edwina was not for him. He felt that he did not want a wife who would be so very much richer than he. His chosen profession was the Navy and it was one where, as he said, not only were money and position no help in furthering his career, but they were positive hindrances.

An energetic and adventurous young man, he agreed to accompany his cousin and close friend, the Prince of Wales (later Edward VIII) on his second Commonwealth tour. They visited India, a country Louis was destined to love for the rest of his life, and went to stay in Delhi. Edwina, however, had no intention of letting the matter of her vast fortune stand in the way of her happiness. Knowing that Dickie was as much in love with her as she with him, she borrowed £100 and bought a one-way ticket to India, showing a resourcefulness that was to become one of her best-loved characteristics. She went to stay with the Viceroy and, at a Vice-regal ball on St Valentine's Day in 1922, between dances four and six, Louis asked her to marry him. She accepted immediately and the couple promptly began to make arrangements.

The Prince of Wales sent a telegram to the King, requesting his royal permission for the marriage and Louis wrote to his mother, his father having died in the previous year. The Viceroy also wrote a letter to Edwina's aunt, saying that there was nothing to be done as Edwina was clearly very much in love and that, although Lord Louis was a good-looking young man, 'I only wish she could marry someone with better career prospects in front of him.' The Viceroy can be forgiven for not realizing what the future held in store for the Mountbattens: in 1922, it didn't look very promising.

Lord Louis had no home of his own, having encouraged his father to sell his German castle in 1920 and having refused to live in a family house on the Isle of Wight because he, a Naval officer, saw no reason for having to catch a boat every time he wanted to go home. After they had become engaged, Edwina told him that she was the heir to Broadlands, a magnificent Georgian mansion in which they lived for many years.

Dickie and Edwina were married on 18 July 1922 and the wedding was a 'right royal' occasion, with the Prince of Wales as best man. After a honeymoon at

Broadlands, Dickie took six months leave at half-pay and he and Edwina visited America, travelling the length and breadth of the continent. The dashing young officer and his lovely and unconventional wife seemed to know everybody. When they visited California, Douglas Fairbanks and Mary Pickford lent their famous home, 'Pickfair', to the newly-weds. It was here that Charlie Chaplin made a short comedy film for Dickie and Edwina, as a wedding present, in which the couple themselves starred.

In 1924, their first daughter, Patricia, was born and her sister, Pamela, followed five years later. Lord Louis' close links with his second cousins were strengthened when his daughters became close friends of Princess Elizabeth and Princess Margaret: the Mountbatten girls later joined the famous Buckingham Palace Girl Guides. Dickie was a stalwart friend

Oblivious to the photographer, Lord Louis stands on the bridge of HMS Kelly *in 1940.*

The Mountbattens' friendship with Ghandi smoothed the path towards an independent India.

and outspoken adviser to both Edward VIII and the Duke of York (later George VI) during the Abdication crisis and offered real comfort and support to the new King.

In July 1939 he accompanied the royal family on a visit to Dartmouth, where he and King George shared memories of their naval training. It was on this visit that he introduced Princess Elizabeth to his nephew, Prince Philip of Greece, the son of his sister, Princess Alice. The young Prince, now a naval cadet, had been raised and educated under the guardianship of his uncle, George, the second Marquess of Milford Haven, until his death in 1938. Uncle Dickie then took over the role of mentor and, when Prince Philip became a naturalized British subject before his marriage to Princess Elizabeth, he took the name Mountbatten as a compliment to his two uncles.

Some two months later, Britain was at war. Lord Louis became commander of the 5th Destroyer Flotilla, operating from HMS *Kelly*, still remembered as a happy and well-disciplined ship. In December 1939, the *Kelly* was mined just off the north-east coast of England; and no sooner was she repaired and back in action than she was under fire from the air off the coast of Germany for four days and nights. Lord Louis refused to scuttle her and she somehow limped into port. A photograph taken at this time shows him on the bridge, one hand in his pocket, looking as urbane and nonchalant as if posing in a studio. In fact, the picture was taken by one of the crew without his knowledge, and at a time when it seemed that both the subject and the picture were doomed to a watery grave.

When he was awarded the Distinguished Service Order, his mother commented, 'It is a good thing that he did not get it until everybody had read the details. . . . Now no one can in fairness say that he has not earned it.' Noel Coward's famous film, *In Which We Serve*, was based on the story of the *Kelly*. The ship was eventually sunk by German dive-bombers off the coast of Crete in 1941. Lord Louis was the last to leave the ship and, typically, was responsible for mustering the survivors, getting them into the boats and raising their morale.

Winston Churchill, as Minister of Defence as well as Prime Minister, knew better than to continue to endanger the life of one of the few great military leaders in those dark days. He put him in charge of Combined Operations, a vital and prestigious job, organizing operations into German-occupied Europe. Nevertheless, it annoyed Louis Mountbatten because, no matter how grand, it was an office job and he was a man of action. At the Quebec Conference in 1943, attended by Churchill and US President Roosevelt, he cultivated Churchill's friendship in the hope of being sent to sea again and he could not understand why his request was evaded.

The explanation was that Churchill needed him elsewhere. After two years of successful work in Combined Operations, he was offered the job of Supreme Commander in South-East Asia. He had no doubts that he was the right man to undertake this staggering responsibility. As he himself put it at the time, 'I have a congenital weakness for feeling certain that I can do anything.'

And he could, though not without controversy dogging his tracks. His public image as a glamorous and good-looking royal playboy was very much at odds with the reality of the hardworking professional. He accepted the fact that anyone as ruthless as he considered himself to be would make enemies and got on with the job. He took charge of one million men of mixed nationalities in the 'forgotten army' fighting in South-East Asia. The Japanese appeared to be invincible, the monsoons made combat practically impossible for part of the year and malaria and dysentery were rife. Always decisive and imaginative in his approach, Lord Louis restored morale, organized campaigns throughout the monsoon season and called in teams of doctors.

He was one of the major figures in the final surrender of Japan and all his life kept the symbolic sword as a memento: the Japanese supremo in South-East Asia, Field Marshal Count Terauchi, had felt that handing over his own service sword was an insufficient gesture for the humiliation of defeat and sent to Tokyo for a priceless heirloom, the blade of which had been forged in 1292. When it was suggested that he should return this legendary weapon after the formal ceremony, Lord Mountbatten replied, 'Not bloody likely!'

Edwina, who had been made Superintendent-in-Chief of the voluntary medical organization, the St John Ambulance Brigade, devoted her tireless energy to the welfare of former prisoners-of-war of the Japanese and her work was heroic. By 1945, she and her husband had most certainly cleared the Battenberg name and brought honour to that of Mountbatten.

In 1947, Lord Louis was created Earl Mountbatten of Burma and in the same year he was sworn in as Viceroy of India. It was an impressive ceremony, and although he was not overawed, he found it, as he said, '. . . a sobering thought that I now had to guide the destinies of one-fifth of humanity'. In fact, he was to guide those millions through the tricky period immediately preceding independence from British rule. His attitude was typically straightforward—to guide a people, you must know them—and he did, very well. He saw his task not as a winding up of affairs in the last days of an old colony, but as the establishment of a new and independent state.

He was made Viceroy at the suggestion of Clement Attlee, the British Prime Minister, who recognized Mountbatten's administrative abilities and deep sympathy for and understanding of national aspirations as unique qualifications for this testing task. Earl Mountbatten insisted on, and was granted, two conditions before he agreed to the appointment. First, he must be allowed to return to the Navy at his correct rank when his work in India was completed and, second, he must be given absolute powers to perform that work.

With Edwina by his side, he returned to that same house where that previous Viceroy had ironically written his letter twenty-five years earlier, wishing that Edwina would marry a man with better career prospects. Among the Mountbattens' greatest friends were two of India's most famous men, Pandit Nehru, the nationalist politician, and Mahatma Ghandi. It was through them that the Mountbattens' presence in those difficult times was not only acceptable but seen to be so. Ghandi who, for religious reasons, was never photographed eating or drinking, relaxed the rule so that he could be photographed while taking a light breakfast with Lord Louis in the grounds of their house in Delhi. When Ghandi heard of the wedding plans of Prince Philip and Princess Elizabeth, he was delighted but regretted that he had nothing to send as a wedding present, as his only possessions were a loincloth and a cheap watch. The Mountbattens suggested that he make the Princess a present on his spinning wheel. A piece of cloth, made from thread he had spun himself, was duly dispatched and is now one of the

Queen's most treasured possessions, although her grandmother, Queen Mary, was shocked and insisted that it was an insult.

It was Uncle Dickie, the 'royal troubleshooter', who had earlier handled the problem of public response to the news of the Princess's engagement. Anti-foreign feeling was still very strong in Britain and there was some anxiety that the newly-named Lieutenant Mountbatten might meet with disfavour because of his European connections, particularly his German ones. Lord Louis consulted the press barons of Fleet Street a month before the announcement was made and cleverly manoeuvred them into a position which made it impossible for them to raise difficulties later.

The date fixed by the British Government for independence in India was June 1948. Mountbatten recognized the impatience in the mood of the country and persuaded the British Government to bring the date forward to August 1947. He was, in fact, Viceroy for only five months but stayed on as Governor-General at the request of Pandit Nehru. The partition of the country into the separate states of India and Pakistan resulted in widespread rioting between Hindus and Moslems. The violent conflict created thousands upon thousands of refugees and where they were, there was Edwina Mountbatten. If her actions in South-East Asia had been magnificent, in India she surpassed even her own high standards of service and compassion, devoting all her time and immense energy to the care of refugees.

Dickie and Edwina returned to London in 1948. He was anxious to resume his career in the Navy: the Admiralty were unenthusiastic, feeling that a man who had been Supreme Allied Commander and Viceroy of India would not fit easily into naval hierarchy, but he did return to the service he loved and also to the Mediterranean. He became successively Commander-in-Chief Mediterranean, Commander-in-Chief NATO Mediterranean and, in 1955, First Sea Lord, bringing back honour to his father's memory once and for all. In 1958 he was appointed Chief of the Defence Staff and oversaw a project he had long planned—to reform the service ministries.

Edwina gave him her unflagging support and, at the same time, kept her active interest in the St John Ambulance Brigade. Her rank of Superintendent-in-Chief was no mere honorary title in Britain any more than it had been abroad. The uniform didn't just come out of mothballs for special ceremonies. On the contrary, for much of her life she lived in it and she certainly lived for it.

In 1960, she began a punishing tour of the Far East on behalf of the St John Ambulance Brigade, immediately after the wedding of her younger daughter, Lady Pamela, to the interior designer, David Hicks. Just four days later, she was dead. Dickie received over six thousand telegrams and messages of condolence from all over the world, from kings, heads of state and ordinary people, who all claimed friendship with his wife. With her capacity for compassion, it was quite believable.

At her own request, she was buried at sea, in traditional naval fashion. This moving ceremony took place just off Portsmouth from the deck of HMS *Wakeful*, accompanied, at the request of the Indian Government, by the Indian frigate *Trishul*. Dickie cast his wreath on the waters and stood silently gazing after it. He said later that the death of Edwina was the 'one great blow' in his life and that 'it is impossible to overestimate what she did'.

He never ceased to miss the loving comfort and support of a wife who had shared so wholeheartedly in his own busy and eventful life. Nevertheless, he gladly continued to give his services wherever they were needed. Even after his retirement in 1955, he was the chairman of a number of royal commissions and served on many educational committees.

In 1979, he and his family were on holiday in Sligo in the Republic of Ireland, staying at the castle where he had spent his summers for the past thirty-five years. On 27 August he set out in the yacht *Shadow V* with his elder daughter and son-in-law, Lord Brabourne, their sons, Nicholas and Timothy, and Lord Brabourne's mother. They had only just left the shore when an IRA terrorist bomb exploded, killing Earl Mountbatten and his grandson, Nicholas, instantly. The royal family, world statesmen, men who had served under his command and ordinary people were all deeply shocked and distressed by the violent death of a man whose skill, integrity, imagination and sympathy had endeared him to millions. The Indian Government declared a period of mourning for seven days. A service was held at Westminster Abbey, attended by the royal family. He was privately interred, at his own wish, in Romsey Abbey near Broadlands, the beautiful home he had shared with his beloved Edwina.

Lord Mountbatten, three months before his tragic death, walking in the grounds of his beloved Broadlands, the magnificent Georgian home he shared with Edwina.

Queen Elizabeth 11
&
Prince Philip

Elizabeth and Philip

One of the Duke of York's major concerns during the critical period of decision before Edward VIII's abdication in December 1936 was the burden he would be placing on the young shoulders of his elder daughter, Princess Elizabeth as Heir Presumptive and future Queen.

He was not alone in this worry for there was concern in political circles about future public feeling for the monarchy if the abdication became a reality. Some felt that it would be better to select the youngest of the royal brothers, the lively and handsome George, Duke of Kent, rather than the shy and modest Duke of York. In addition, George was the only one of the brothers with a son to become the Prince of Wales and it was thought that a male heir would be better able to cope with the especially heavy responsibilities which the Abdication crisis had caused and to re-establish public affection and respect for the monarchy.

On Friday, 11 December 1936, Parliament ratified the Instrument of Abdication, the Duke of York became King George VI and the ten-year-old Princess Elizabeth became heir to the throne. The events preceding his accession saddened the King both as a private man and as a public figure. Impelled by a deep sense of duty inherited from his parents, the King applied himself to his new role and this could not help but shape the Princess's attitudes and views of her future role during the formative years of her adolescence.

In February 1937, the King and his family moved from 145 Piccadilly, one of London's main thoroughfares, to the royal apartments at Buckingham Palace. Both the King and Queen were determined to continue to bring up their daughters as ordinary little girls as far as possible, while at the same time preparing Princess Elizabeth for her future. The Princess was in many ways a rather serious, self-sufficient child and her life was necessarily secluded. Opportunities for making friends were limited, although, of course, there was never any lack of invitations. Her days revolved around the companionship of parents, her sister, Margaret MacDonald her nurserymaid whom she called Bobo, and Marion Crawford, her governess, known to the Princesses as Crawfie.

Everywhere the young Princesses went they were followed by an army of reporters and photographers and, as a result, Princess Elizabeth learned quickly to control any outward show of the normal spontaneous

reactions of a little girl. The Duke and Duchess of York had treated their two daughters alike, even dressing them in identical clothes, and only making those distinctions between them that a four-year age-gap would require in any family. As King and Queen they decided to continue this policy as far as possible and to avoid any suggestions of rivalry or inequality between the two children. For their father's coronation, for example, they wore identical robes and coronets. A deep bond of lasting affection between the Queen and Princess Margaret has since weathered many storms.

The family had always been close and loving and, even with their new responsibilities, the King and Queen still spent as much time as possible with their daughters. The King himself supervised the arrangements for their education. He introduced politics and political personalities to Princess Elizabeth through the humorous pages of the magazine *Punch* as well as through the more serious columns of *The Times* newspaper. The Queen, with her own special brand of charm and poise, encouraged her daughters to acquire the qualities so closely identified with her—perfect manners, elegance and good deportment. Queen Mary undertook to teach her granddaughters about art.

Life in the palace was not always serious and full of responsibilities. The King and Queen loved family life and really enjoyed the fun and games they shared with their two lively and active daughters. The King had a tremendous sense of fun and delighted in the romps, charades and parlour games.

Princess Elizabeth celebrated her thirteenth birthday at Windsor in April 1939. Naturally earnest and conscientious, she lacked the strain of devilment which characterized her younger sister. She had inherited much of her adored father's personality and modelled herself on him. Serious, shy, immature, inexperienced, and perhaps a little young for her age, she began her holidays the following summer with a family cruise along the south coast of Britain on the royal yacht *Victoria and Albert.*

On 22 July, the royal family sailed up the River Dart to visit the Royal Naval College, set on a hill above the Devonshire town of Dartmouth. For the Princesses it was an exciting break from the secluded and familiar routine of schoolroom life at Buckingham Palace or the Royal Lodge, Windsor. With the royal visitors on board the yacht was Lord Louis Mountbatten. A naval man himself, he had telephoned his old friend, the college commander, to suggest that his nephew, Prince Philip of Greece, who was a naval

cadet there, would be a good choice to act as royal escort. As a Prince in his own right, he was used to mixing with royalty and wouldn't be overawed.

Princess Elizabeth was at a rather awkward, in-between age and still very much a schoolgirl. Prince Philip was a tall, slim, self-confident eighteen. The gap was wide, not just in age but in experience of the world, yet this was the meeting which would change both their lives. (They may, in fact, have met before as Prince Philip had attended the marriage of his cousin Princess Marina to the Duke of Kent in 1934 and been a family guest at the coronation of King George VI in 1937. Apparently, the young people had made no great impression on each other on either of these occasions.)

The scene was set for this momentous meeting when the *Victoria and Albert* arrived at Dartmouth. But, as a foretaste of the difficulties the future would bring them, an unexpected problem almost caused the visit to be cancelled. That evening the college authorities contacted the royal party to inform them that there was an outbreak of both chickenpox and mumps at the college. Elizabeth and Margaret, eagerly anticipat-

Smiling their delight during a visit to the Royal Naval College in 1939, the royal family did not know that the handsome young cadet, Prince Philip of Greece (second from right), had captured forever the heart of the 13-year-old Elizabeth (second from left).

ing the next day's excitements, were crestfallen at the thought of being left on board the yacht. Rather than disappoint them, their parents decided that they would be allowed to go.

Next day, in blue dresses with matching coats, the Princesses accompanied their parents ashore. The two girls were dispatched to amuse themselves at the house of the college commander, Admiral Sir Frederick Dalrymple-Hamilton. It was here that Philip met them but accounts differ about exactly where in the house this happened. The weather was changeable and while it was raining the Princesses played with a clockwork railway in the nursery. Later they played croquet in the garden and certainly Philip had joined them by then.

The tall, blonde, blue-eyed Prince, looking exceedingly smart is his cadet uniform, must have made a striking impression on the two young schoolgirls. Princess Elizabeth, according to Crawfie, especially admired the way he could jump. He didn't seem to pay any special attention to her and, in fact, spent a lot of time teasing her sister. He spent the rest of the day escorting them round the college and grounds and generally entertaining them. In the evening he and other cadets went aboard the royal yacht to attend a dinner given by the King. The Princesses were not present. Keeping to their normal routine, they had gone to bed but the next day they again went ashore and met Philip, who continued his escort duties.

When the time came for the *Victoria and Albert* to raise anchor, a flotilla of small boats from the college gathered nearby and followed the yacht out of the bay. As the yacht gathered speed, one by one the boats fell back, until just one remained. Philip continued to row after the yacht until the King became anxious for his safety. The signal to turn back was flying from the mast but Philip would not see it. At last the King called for a megaphone and finally Philip obeyed the order to return, shouted perhaps by the King or else by Lord Louis Mountbatten. Motionless, Princess Elizabeth followed the boat's progress through her father's binoculars until it was out of sight.

A few months later, Britain was at war. The Princesses were in Scotland when war was declared and it was decided to leave them there until Christmas, which was spent at Sandringham with the King and Queen. After Christmas, the children moved to Windsor where they spent the remaining years of the war. At the Queen's request, Crawfie maintained as normal a routine of lessons, walks and rides as possible. The King and Queen considered evacuating their daughters to a place of safety outside Britain but rejected the idea. The Queen is reported as saying, 'The children won't leave without me; I won't leave without the King; and the King will never leave.' So, from 1939 to 1945, Princess Elizabeth lived a life even more secluded and restricted than before. The demands on her parents' time were immense and she saw far less of them than she or they would have liked. The daily routine continued to revolve around the little circle of female companions, Princess Margaret, Bobo and Crawfie.

Prince Philip, meanwhile, was on active service on the battleship HMS *Valiant* in the Mediterranean. In March 1941, the *Valiant* was badly holed in the battle

The King and Queen spent as much time as possible with their daughters. Enjoying simple pastimes and each other's company, they were a truly loving family.

of Matapan and Philip, who had manned a searchlight under heavy fire, was mentioned in dispatches.

One of the diversions the Princesses threw themselves into in a bid to relieve the monotony was the annual Christmas pantomime. Naval duties had prevented Prince Philip from seeing earlier productions, but in 1943 he was able to accept the King and Queen's invitation to spend the holiday at Windsor. News of the addition to the guest list must have added spice to the rehearsals of *Aladdin* for at least one member of the cast. During the performance no one laughed louder than Philip at the antics on the stage and Crawfie was particularly struck with the sparkle and animation of Princess Elizabeth's performance.

As the King watched, something gave him the first clue that the feeling between the Prince and his daughter was more than a simple boy and girl friendship. To test the Princess, the King waited until Philip was out of the room and then made a joke about him. To his consternation, Elizabeth blushed a deep red, but said nothing.

The Queen was worried by her daughter's strong feelings for Philip. She felt that, at only seventeen, she was too young to know her own mind. This was the first deep attachment she had formed. Could she know if this were true love or the infatuation of a rather shy girl from a sheltered background for a handsome, outgoing young man? The years of war had prevented her from enjoying the normally busy social life and carefree, light-hearted romances of most young girls. Her companions had been almost exclusively female and she had had little opportunity to meet young men. In March 1944, the King wrote, 'We both think she is too young for that now as she has never met any young men of her own age.'

Both the King and Queen liked Philip and felt that he had all the attributes to make him a suitable consort for a future Queen. But no one knew better than they the exceptional demands that marriage to a monarch entailed. They had been blessed with a specially happy marriage and they wanted the same for their daughter. The penalties that a wrong choice of partner would bring were too terrible to contemplate and the matter of his brother and Wallis Simpson was never far below the surface of the King's mind throughout his reign. The Prince and Princess must wait. If time and wartime separations did not sever the bonds, then the matter could be considered again.

In due course, the war ended and the King and Queen were anxious to re-establish the family life they had known before 1939. The days were packed with shooting, fishing, picnics and other country pastimes. But even a king cannot turn back the clock and by this time Elizabeth was twenty, no longer a child but a young woman with a surprising streak of independence and toughness. She placed a photograph of Prince Philip in a prominent place on the mantelpiece in her sitting room and soon rumours of romance began to appear in the newspapers. In fact, the press speculated on a number of possible suitors.

The King started giving private dances at Buckingham Palace and invited suitable companions for the Princesses to tea and for weekends at Windsor or Sandringham. Queen Mary was secretly amused by what she considered the King's unsubtle plans to encourage eligible young men to surround the Princess on every possible occasion.

Philip's holiday at Balmoral in August 1946 seems to have been the turning point. The King and Queen had to acknowledge that their daughter was truly in love. Even though the couple had parental consent at this point, there were serious problems to be sorted out centring on Philip's Greek nationality. He could not marry the Princess without adopting British nationality but the political situation in Greece was exceptionally difficult. Earlier, there had been doubts as to whether the Greek monarchy would be restored. The British Government decided to postpone Philip's naturalization until after the Greek general election and plebiscite on the monarchy planned for March 1946, in case it should be interpreted as an official indication of their political stance. The plebiscite resulted in a majority in favour of the monarchy but this still didn't help Philip. The British Government now felt that it would be undiplomatic for a member of the Greek royal family to renounce his nationality so close to the restoration.

There was nothing the young couple could do but wait. Nevertheless, they became privately engaged. No public announcement was made because of the nationality problem. The King and Queen also felt that the couple still needed time to be sure of their feelings. In September 1946 a statement was issued from Buckingham Palace, denying rumours of an engagement.

Although Philip's nationality was Greek, he was, in fact, a member of the royal house of Denmark, the Schleswig-Holstein-Sonderberg-Glucksburgs. Prince William of Denmark had been invited to take the Greek throne in 1863 and had then taken the name of

King George I of Greece. Prince Philip, his direct descendant, had been born on 10 June 1921 on the island of Corfu. The Greek throne proved to be very unstable. George I, Philip's grandfather, was assassinated in 1913; Constantine I, Philip's uncle, deposed in 1917 and later restored to the throne, abdicated in 1922; and George II, Philip's cousin, abdicated in 1923, was restored to the throne in 1935, expelled in 1941 and restored again after the plebiscite in 1946.

During one of the earlier periods of unrest, the baby Prince Philip had left Greece in an improvised cot made of orange crates on a British light cruiser in 1922. His father, Prince Andrew, had been rescued from threat of execution in Athens by the direct intervention of King George V.

Prince Philip was the youngest child of Prince Andrew and Princess Alice of Battenberg. His four sisters were considerably older than he and while he was still quite young, his parents drifted apart. Prince Andrew moved to Monte Carlo, leaving his wife with the sole responsibility for their young son.

Princess Alice was the youngest daughter of Prince Louis of Battenberg, the sister of Lord Louis Mountbatten, and a great-granddaughter of Queen Victoria. She turned to her brothers for help and the elder, George, made himself responsible for his nephew's education and care until his death in 1938. He sent Philip to preparatory school at Cheam in England and then to Salem School in Bavaria, Germany. Kurt Hahn, former adviser to Prince Max of Bavaria, had founded the school in 1920 as an experiment to combine the best of British and German teaching methods and character building. By 1933, the school was world famous and the fact that Prince Philip's second sister, Theodora, was married to the Margrave of Baden, made it a particularly good choice. By the time Prince Philip arrived, Kurt Hahn had been imprisoned because of his opposition to Nazism. After his release, negotiated by the British politician, Ramsay MacDonald, he moved his school to a house called Gordonstoun in Morayshire in Scotland. Prince Philip became a pupil at the new school, demonstrating fine qualities of leadership and responding well to challenge. Less praiseworthy were his tendencies to impatience and intolerance.

After the death of his Uncle George, Philip came under the wing of his younger uncle, Lord Louis Mountbatten, known to the family as Dickie. When Philip's naturalization finally came through, he adopted the name Mountbatten—a graceful compliment to the two men who had been his mentors since his early childhood.

The King had planned a visit to South Africa in 1947 and it was decided that the royal tour would go ahead. Prince Philip's name was not included on the list of the royal party and newspaper speculation about a royal romance died down. It was during this tour that news of her future husband's naturalization reached Princess Elizabeth.

The Princess celebrated her twenty-first birthday on 21 April 1947, in Cape Town. The occasion was marked by a broadcast to the Commonwealth in which the Princess said, 'I declare before you all that my whole life, whether it be long or short, shall be devoted to your service.' It was an awe-inspiring thought for a future husband to contemplate.

On 9 July 1947, the press was given an announcement for publication after midnight. It said,

> *'It is with great pleasure that the King and Queen announce the betrothal of their dearly beloved daughter the Princess Elizabeth to Lieutenant Philip Mountbatten RN, son of the late Prince Andrew of Greece and Princess Andrew (Princess Alice of Battenberg) to which union the King has gladly given his consent.'*

As the news spread, crowds began to gather outside the Palace hoping for a glimpse of the happy couple. As they waited they sang 'All the nice girls love a sailor.'

The hardships endured by the British people during the war years were far from over in 1947. These were the grey days of severe rationing in peacetime. The most brutal winter of the century had made existing food and fuel crises even more desperate. In this grim climate of austerity, the romantic wedding of the popular Princess and her handsome sailor was, indeed, as Winston Churchill observed, 'a flash of colour on the hard road we have to travel'.

The announcement of the engagement on 10 July was rapturously received by the public but it left a scant four-and-a-half months for preparations for the great day. The courtship had been exceptionally long, in spite of the bride's youth, and the couple were impatient to marry now all the obstacles confronting them were overcome.

The royal family felt that an ostentatious display would be inappropriate in this age of austerity, so the decorations and banqueting traditional to such an

important event were restrained. But the bridal gown for the future Queen had to be very special indeed.

The designer, the late Norman Hartnell, flung himself into a whirl of frenzied activity. He cancelled a trip to the United States, where he was to receive a prestigious award, to seek inspiration for a design in London's art galleries. In the National Gallery he found the answer—a 'Botticelli figure in clinging ivory silk, trailed with jasmine, similax, syringa and small white blossoms'. His design approved, Mr Hartnell whitewashed the windows of his workshop to preserve secrecy and set his design studio manager to sleep on a camp bed by the work in progress, to protect the Princess's dress from the inquisitive eyes of the press and would-be imitators.

The resulting creation was exquisitely beautiful—ivory duchess satin, cut on classic lines, with a fitted bodice, long, tight sleeves and a full, falling skirt. The heart-shaped neckline was embroidered with seed pearls and crystal in a delicate floral design. Pearl-embroidered star flowers formed a pointed waistline and embroidery of raised seed pearls on the swirling skirt represented garlands of white York roses and wheat. Bands of orange blossom and star flowers formed a border around the hem, appliquéd with transparent tulle edged with seed pearls and crystal.

Silk for the full court train, four and a half metres (fifteen feet) long, came from an English silk-worm farm. The transparent ivory silk tulle fell from the shoulders, edged with satin flowers and appliquéd with satin star flowers, roses and wheat, encrusted with pearls and crystal embroidery. The bridal veil of crisp white tulle was held in place by a pearl and diamond tiara from the Crown Jewels. The bride's sandals of ivory duchess satin were finished with silver buckles studded with small pearls.

As the day of the wedding approached, Londoners revelled in the unfamiliar festive atmosphere. Decorations were confined to a small area, but the route from the Palace to Westminster Abbey was gaily decked with flags and bunting. Yellow and white banners appliquéd with wine-coloured motifs bearing the initials 'E' and 'P' were mounted on blue masts in front of the Palace. A plaster front was built inside the Abbey to conceal newsreel cameras.

The day of the wedding, 20 November 1947, saw the route lined with many thousands of people. Parlia-

The happy couple on their wedding day in 1947. The gorgeous bridal gown, specially designed for the future Queen, had a full court train.

Passing through Admiralty Arch, the bridal procession celebrated both a royal wedding and the post-war return of spectacular ceremony.

ment Square was jammed solid with spectators and thousands more pressed up to the gates of Buckingham Palace.

Inside the Palace, the last minutes before setting out were at least as fraught as those for any bride. The tiara broke as it was being placed on the Princess's head and a jeweller raced away to repair it. Meanwhile, a secretary was desperately fighting his way through the crowds with the pearls the Princess was to wear. They were a wedding gift from her parents and had been on display with the other presents at St James's Palace. The bride's bouquet of white orchids was temporarily mislaid and discovered at the last minute in a refrigerator. The Princess was described as having her head in the clouds but the Queen calmly kept things organized.

The procession to the Abbey was on schedule. For the first time since September 1939, the Household Cavalry appeared in full ceremonial dress. The sudden glamorous spectacle after so many terrible

Waiting crowds were thrilled with this glimpse of the popular and romantic new Duke and Duchess of Edinburgh.

years triggered passionate emotions in the waiting crowds. They broke into cheers which didn't cease throughout the procession and rose to a wave of jubilant roaring at the sight of the Princess and the King.

The Queen and Princess Margaret led the pageant in the Glass Coach with a Captain's Escort of two officers and thirty-two other ranks on sleek black horses. The Life Guards riding in front of the coach wore red tunics with black collars and white plumes. Following the coaches rode the Royal Horse Guards in blue tunics with red collars and plumes. Behind them rode the Scandinavian and Greek royal guests in carriages.

Queen Mary's car led the motor-car procession, followed by the rest of the foreign royalty and the Duke and Duchess of Gloucester. Finally came the King and his radiant daughter in the Irish Coach with the Sovereign's Escort, consisting of seven officers and 119 other ranks.

Inside the Abbey, at the centre of the majestic procession of officials, the King's Scholars, the choir, the clergy, the bridesmaids and other attendants, was the slight figure of the bride on the arm of her beaming father. The Princess's small cousins, Prince William of Gloucester and Prince Michael of Kent, in white shirts and tartan kilts, bore her train.

Many of the guests at the ceremony bore witness to the fact that this was a brief flash of brightness in a bleak time. Peers and peeresses of the realm had to dispense with Court robes after the war and many of the men had to wear lounge suits instead of morning dress. Ladies in simple morning dresses and hats wore medals for service to the Empire in place of jewels.

Among those present at the Princess's personal invitation were twenty girls who had helped to make her wedding dress, her former riding instructress, the schoolmistress of Birkhall, Aberdeenshire, where part of the honeymoon was to be spent and the station-master from Wolferton, Norfolk, the station for the royal estate at Sandringham.

All weddings are emotional occasions but at this wedding a whole nation felt that it was their daughter

Royal tours are not all hard work and strict formality. The royal couple, in traditional dress, swing their partners with a will in a Canadian Square Dance in 1951.

marrying the dashing young Prince who had so distinguished himself in the war that had just been won. The bride's proud father felt a deep and more personal emotion. He later wrote to the Princess,

> *'I was so proud of you and thrilled at having you so close to me on our long walk in Westminster Abbey, but when I handed your hand to the Archbishop I felt that I had lost something very precious. You were so calm and composed during the service and said your words with such conviction.'*

Sparing a thought for all the recent misery and the defiant courage of her country, and never forgetting the significance of her position, even at her happiest moment, Princess Elizabeth sent her bouquet to be laid on the tomb of the Unknown Warrior before emerging from the Abbey into the sunshine.

The wedding breakfast was modest by royal standards. One hundred and fifty guests in the white and gold supper room of Buckingham Palace had a light meal of sole, partridge and ice cream while pipers from Balmoral and the string band of the Grenadier Guards played to them. The room was decorated with pink carnations sent by the British Carnation Society and a sprig of white heather from Balmoral was placed beside each plate. The small centre table for the eight main members of the family was decorated with sprigs of myrtle taken from a bush raised from myrtle in Queen Victoria's wedding bouquet. Speeches were brief.

Throughout the afternoon the dense throngs outside the Palace called for the couple, bringing them out on to the balcony three times. As darkness fell, they emerged from the Palace. The Princess wore a

The Queen and Prince Philip have always made time to relax with their four children. Proud parents, they are in complete agreement on the importance of family life.

simple going-away outfit of mist-blue crepe with a matching velour hat. At the end of the day's solemnity and magnificence, the bridesmaids, led by the radiantly beautiful Princess Margaret, just seventeen, gave an informal send-off to the newlyweds as they left for their honeymoon. They gathered up their long skirts and with the King and Queen heading a crowd of guests, they dashed across the Palace courtyard to shower the young couple with handfuls of rose petals as they drove away. In the end it was just like the last moments of any wedding party. Parents, relatives and high-spirited friends ran after the coach, calling their goodbyes and good wishes to the young people as they set off in life together.

The fairy-tale wedding and the honeymoon were but an interval in this enduring love-story. The newly-created Duke of Edinburgh planned to continue his naval career in the tradition of the Mountbatten family, while playing a supportive role to his young wife, the heir to the throne. Princess Elizabeth, whose radiant happiness was apparent to all who saw her, continued working closely with her beloved father, while taking a keen interest in her husband's naval duties. Parenthood came as a joy to both of them. By the time Prince Charles and Princess Anne had arrived, the Princess was still under twenty-five and the Duke of Edinburgh under thirty. They looked forward to a youthful family life, unfettered by the full responsibilities of monarchy.

Unhappily, the declining health of King George

A fine horsewoman herself, the Queen laughs and chats with her daughter and son-in-law at Badminton—a thoroughly modern and informal mother and monarch.

Huge crowds in Australia give a heartening welcome to the royal couple on their Jubilee visit to celebrate twenty-five years as monarch and consort.

brought them more than natural anxiety for him. Princess Elizabeth was required to take on more and more responsibility. Inexperienced and nervous, she turned to her husband for help and support. And so, far earlier than they had imagined, the Duke of Edinburgh was faced with the choice of pursuing his own ambitions or abandoning them for ever to help his wife in this difficult time. The Princess's choice of husband may have been made when she was young and inexperienced, but now it became clear just how much wisdom she had shown. Philip fully understood where the duty undertaken in their marriage now lay. Less than four years after their wedding, he took permanent leave from the Navy. It was a hard blow and a heavy sacrifice for a proud man and fine officer.

Less than a year later, the Duke broke the news of her father's death to his wife—news which meant that Princess Elizabeth Alexandra Mary was now Queen of Great Britain, her Dominions and her Possessions beyond the Seas and that the Duke of Edinburgh had become the Queen's consort.

In the years which followed Prince Philip has had to face many situations which would be ego-deflating for many a man. In these days of awakening sexual equality, women of achievement and position are no longer such a rarity but the Queen and Prince Philip came from a conservative and tradition-bound milieu, where a husband's position was generally considered more important.

A man like Philip cannot have borne with complete equanimity the fact that, after her succession to the throne, the Queen and her children were to be known by the name Windsor rather than Mountbatten; that should the Queen have died before Prince Charles became of age, Princess Margaret, not he, would have become Regent and guardian to the heir; that his restless ego and breezy extroversion had to be controlled to meet the endless demands of tedious schedules and protocol.

The Queen has always been a meticulous, controlled type of person, while Prince Philip is by nature easy-going, impatient, restless and extroverted, sometimes to the point of indiscretion. According to rumour, there have been occasions when—as in most loving marriages—they have not been on speaking terms with each other. Palace staff are said to describe them as 'two acid drops' when they are in this mood.

The Queen has little time for interests and hobbies outside her work and her children. Her consuming passion is for racing, riding and breeding horses, which Philip finds boring. He himself has a keen interest in photography, painting, model-making and design, as well as being a fine sportsman. She likes very plain food, while he relishes sophisticated cooking when he is away from home.

But, as with all good and lasting marriages, their differences complement each other and their life together is basically balanced, happy and cosy. Only with each other can they share private jokes and are known to laugh uproariously and talk eagerly non-stop with each other.

Romance has not faded with the onset of middle age. On wedding anniversaries, whether they are together or in different parts of the world, Prince Philip always sends his wife a bouquet of her favourite white orchids to remind her of her bridal bouquet.

The essential strength of the partnership may be attributed to a mutual respect and concern for each other. The Queen has tried over the years to give her husband a role he can make uniquely his own, tuned to his special strengths and abilities. In addition, she has found ways to eliminate some of the anomalies in their public relationship. In October 1952, she announced that, except when prevented by Act of Parliament, Philip should 'have, hold and enjoy Place, Pre-eminence and Precedence next to Her Majesty'. In 1953, she caused the Regency Act to be amended so that, in the event of their son becoming King before he was of age, her husband would be his guardian and Regent. In 1957, in addition to the titles bestowed by King George VI at their wedding, including the Duke of Edinburgh, she gave him the title Prince. Finally, in 1960, shortly before the birth of Prince Andrew, she declared that her descendants should have the surname Mountbatten-Windsor.

For his part, Prince Philip has always been seen to be the Queen's staunchest supporter in her role as monarch. Sometimes a blunt, outspoken man, his harshest flare-ups have always been directed at critics of the Queen. While he is famous for his relaxed approach and humour, he is quick to lash out at any who dare to be impertinent or familiar about her.

With his encouragement, the Queen has acquired a much more relaxed, easy dignity and a less formal graciousness. The legendary charm and flair of her mother was a difficult example for the Queen to follow. She took after her shy father and Prince Philip's dash has done wonders in bringing out her confidence, warmth and humour.

Away from the public spotlight, Prince Philip is very much the head of the family. After his own unsettled childhood, he was determined to provide a constant and strong fatherly influence for his children. He and the Queen are in complete agreement on the importance of family life and she looks to him in the upbringing of their family. When Prince Charles was sent to his father's old school, Gordonstoun, undoubtedly at his father's instigation, many doubts were raised in the press about the unsuitability of the rugged, outdoor approach to education practised at the school for the shy, almost babyish Prince. But time has proved the decision right and Prince Charles looks back to his schooldays with pleasure, convinced that they were spent in precisely the right environment. Prince Philip has encouraged his children to achieve something for themselves and, so far, both Prince Charles and Princess Anne have done so—Charles by achieving a university degree and following a naval career, she with her outstanding skill as a rider.

One of the Queen's most memorable speeches was the one she made on the occasion of her Silver Wedding Anniversary. She wrote it herself and it rang true as an expression of the fulfilment she has found in marriage and family life when she affirmed that 'marriage . . . must be held firm in the web of family relationships between parents and children, between grandparents and grandchildren, between cousins, aunts and uncles.'

It is ironic to recall the doubts expressed in 1936 as to whether Princess Elizabeth would be able to shoulder the responsibilities of being heir to the throne and later Queen. She has earned the love and respect of her subjects as their monarch, and the devotion of her husband, children and wider family: it is indeed a remarkable triumph.

Princess Margaret
&
Peter Townsend

Margaret and Peter

On 21 August 1930, the Duchess of York gave birth to a second daughter at Glamis Castle, her family home in Scotland. Although they were thrilled, the parents had been hoping for a boy and had not considered names for a girl. They thought about christening her Anne Margaret, but the King disliked the name Anne and, in the end, they settled on Margaret Rose. Her four-year-old sister, Princess Elizabeth, delightedly welcomed the newcomer, whom she decided to call 'bud' as 'she's not a real Rose yet'.

The little girls were firm friends from childhood and the Duke and Duchess were determined to make as few distinctions between them as their age-gap permitted. They wore identical clothes, shared lesson times and playtimes and were constant companions. They appeared quite often in public together and everyone who saw them was charmed.

The abdication of 1936 brought major changes in the family's life but the most serious problem for six-year-old Margaret was signing her name. She said, 'I had only just learned how to spell York— Y–O–R–K—and now I am not to use it any more. I am to sign myself Margaret all alone.'

Although the two sisters attended their father's coronation, in identical robes and coronets, and the family moved to Buckingham Palace, the little Princesses' routine carried on much as before. The new King and Queen remained convinced that their daughters should lead lives that were as 'normal' as possible. Unlike today, royal children then led very secluded lives. There was no question of sending them away to school and, in spite of the visits of selected companions and, later, the formation of the Buckingham Palace Girl Guides, Elizabeth and Margaret were, in many ways, lonely and depended on each other for companionship.

Crawfie, their much-loved governess, continued their lessons, and weekends and holidays were spent with their parents on family picnics, games and pastimes at Windsor. George VI was very much a family man and loved to romp and play with his children, particularly the high-spirited Margaret with her well-developed sense of fun. Elizabeth was a rather serious-minded child but Margaret was always a lively bundle of mischief. Particularly bright, she was a devastatingly accurate mimic and gave her father considerable amusement by her imitations of earnest politicians she had overheard on their visits to him.

By 1952, Peter was Margaret's regular escort and the press began to speculate about romance and marriage.

She showed an early interest in music, dance and theatre and was an attentive listener to her grandmother's lectures on antiques and works of art.

Even the years of war from 1939 to 1945 made little difference to the Princesses' way of life. Their activities were more limited but the routine changed little. The King and Queen had many demanding commitments and were unable to spend much time with their children, but otherwise life continued in much the same way as in peacetime.

In spite of their parents' wish to treat their children in exactly the same way, there were inevitable differences between them. Elizabeth was older and consequently allowed a few more privileges, such as a later bedtime, but, more important, she was the Heir Presumptive. Himself ill-prepared for kingship, George VI was determined to ensure that his elder daughter was ready for her future role. In addition, by the time the war came to an end, Elizabeth was grown up and deeply in love with Prince Philip of Greece. Both sisters had, in fact, met the Prince when on holiday in 1939. Although, on that occasion, he spent most of his time amusing the younger Princess, it was the thirteen-year-old Elizabeth's heart he had won. Pleased though she was for her sister, this was obviously something Margaret could not share.

The King and Queen were anxious that Elizabeth's strong and steadfast feeling for Philip might only be the infatuation of a shy and inexperienced girl. Neither of their daughters had had much opportunity to meet suitable young men of their own age. To remedy this, the King arranged a series of private dances for his daughters and many suitable young men were invited to tea parties and for weekend visits to Windsor or Sandringham, the royal estate in Norfolk. The lively and pretty young Margaret, now in her teens, proved a popular companion and thoroughly enjoyed her new and active social life.

Elizabeth's wedding in 1947 was a happy family occasion and Margaret was thrilled by the birth of her nephew, Charles, the following year. Nevertheless, in spite of the constant demand for her company, Margaret must have missed the close companionship of her sister. Her father had been showing signs of illness for some time and was gradually succumbing to cancer. It was an anxious time for the family when the King underwent surgery and one lung was removed. The operation seemed successful but the family knew it was only a postponement of the inevitable. The Queen and Princess Margaret were his constant companions in this trying time and the night before he died

Only four years apart in age, the royal sisters were always good friends and close companions. Elizabeth's marriage in 1947 left a large gap in Margaret's life.

was spent quietly and peacefully with them. His death in February 1952, however much expected, was a shattering blow to his young, impressionable daughter. She had always been exceptionally close to him and she was deeply distressed.

The State funeral, with the whole world's eyes on the bereaved family, was an added strain. Elizabeth, now Queen, had flown back from a tour of Africa. Her own private grief and her new public responsibilities made it difficult for her to give her sister the comfort and support she so badly needed. Their mother, too, though immensely courageous, was overcome with grief at the loss of a husband to whom she was devoted and with whom she had so gladly shared the responsibilities of the sovereign. For Margaret, who was probably the most sensitive member of the family, the strain proved too much and it affected her health. She needed someone to whom she could turn for strength, support and comfort in the same way as her sister could turn to her husband. She found such a man in Group Captain Peter Townsend.

The son of a Lieutenant-Colonel in the British Indian Army, Peter Woolridge Townsend was born in Burma. He was educated in England at Haileybury, a minor public school and then entered the Royal Air Force college at Cranwell. As a pilot, he distinguished himself during World War II, particularly in the Battle of Britain. He is credited with having shot down eleven enemy planes singlehanded and was awarded the Distinguished Flying Cross in 1940. Shortly afterwards, he received the Distinguished Service Order from King George VI at Buckingham Palace.

Towards the end of the war, the King decided to employ a number of young men who had distinguished themselves in battle as temporary equerries. Among these was the charming and efficient ace fighter-pilot, Peter Townsend. He proved to be competent, discreet, obedient and tactful, with the result that he soon became a permanent member of the Royal Household. But, more than this, he became a real friend of the King and his family. As George VI became increasingly ill, he relied more and more on Peter Townsend's efficiency and companionship and, in August 1950, promoted him to Deputy Master of the Household. Throughout the worrying period of the King's last illness, Peter was a constant support to Princess Margaret.

The King and Queen encouraged this friendship and had no thoughts of romantic entanglements. Margaret was the centre of her own circle of friends, 'the Princess Margaret set', bright young people who shared her enthusiasms and interests. But the opportunity for Margaret and Peter to fall in love existed. The strict rules governing the social life of the Princess were relaxed when Peter was her escort. No one thought it at all strange for them to go riding alone together, for example. But Peter Townsend was a very attractive man—'tall, dark and handsome', with remarkably blue eyes. He was also very witty, which undoubtedly appealed to Margaret who was herself renowned for her 'roguishness', as her grandmother, Queen Mary, called it. He was delightfully unstuffy and has been credited with doing much to encourage the more relaxed and out-going post-war royal image.

Margaret could also be impatient with too much protocol and etiquette and welcomed any relaxation of the rules. She was a very attractive young woman who enjoyed dancing, dining and the theatre—in fact, all the pleasant pastimes most young women enjoy, though without causing comment in newspapers or having to obtain official permission. No doubt she enjoyed such social occasions more in the company of an entertaining and good-looking man.

In 1941, Peter had married Rosemary Pawle. As in so many marriages made during wartime, this may have been the result of a romantic impulse to achieve some stability in the chaos of the world. The early years of their married life were disrupted by the separations inevitable for a pilot on active service. When Peter became an equerry to the King, the periods of separation continued. Fortnightly tours of duty and longer trips abroad prevented Peter from spending much time with his family, which, by now, included two sons, Giles and Hugo.

Whether this was the cause, or whether the marriage was never destined to succeed, can only be guessed. Whatever the reason, the couple were divorced in 1952. Peter was the 'innocent' party and was given custody of the children. In fact, by private arrangement, they remained with their mother, who subsequently quietly remarried. In the past, divorce would automatically have required resignation from service in the Royal Household, but the rules were gradually relaxing. The widowed Queen Mother, who appreciated the trustworthiness and friendship Peter had shown her husband, appointed him Comptroller of her new household at Clarence House in London.

Both the Queen Mother and Queen Elizabeth were aware of Margaret's extreme distress after the death of her father and encouraged Peter to divert her from her growing introspection. He took her out on picnics, introduced her to his children and, as he began to restore normality, they fell in love. Sixteen years older than she, this calm, gentle and humorous man must have seemed a tower of strength to Margaret. Her warmth and sympathy were, in turn, welcome comforts to him during the difficult time of his divorce.

It is hard to pinpoint precisely when the rumours linking the Princess and the Group Captain began. Certainly the friendship was splashed across the pages of American newspapers early in 1953. In Britain, the left-wing weekly, *Tribune*, was the first to seize on the subject, not as mere gossip, however, but as a focal point for political discussion.

For many people, even those intimately connected with the royal family, Coronation day was the first time that Margaret's feelings for Peter became obvious. While they were waiting for carriages to take them back to the Palace after the ceremony, guests saw the Queen's sister go up to the Group Captain and pick a thread off his uniform, touching his row of medals with a gesture of loving pride. Only a few months afterwards, the world knew that Princess Margaret, the Queen's sister, was in love with a divorced man.

By July, high government officials, including the

Prime Minister, were holding panic-stricken meetings with the Queen about what came to be called the 'Townsend Affair'. It could no longer be ignored. It is hard to believe today that divorce could be the subject of such scandal and debate as recently as 1953. After all, the mid-1960s saw Government and Royal permission granted for the divorce of the Queen's cousin, the Earl of Harewood. But 1953 was not very far removed in spirit from the drama and strain of the abdication in 1936 and all that it implied. Many of the participants in that upheaval still smarted from the memory, not least of them the Queen Mother and the new Queen. The prospect of a similar scandal in coronation year could not be contemplated.

In addition, there was the legal consideration of the Royal Marriages Act, drawn up in haste in 1772 after a Hanoverian scandal, and still having legal force.

Peter Townsend accompanied the royal party on the South African tour of 1947. Was the pretty 17-year-old Princess already falling in love without knowing it?

This prevents any descendants of George II from marrying without the sovereign's permission while under the age of twenty-five. After this, permission must still be asked but refusal is only binding for one year. The Sovereign is, of course, also temporal Head of the Church of England, which maintained that any marriage solemnized in church could not be dissolved. Consequently, the Queen's hands were tied for she could not give permission for a marriage which the Church would never recognize.

For her, it must have been a painful personal dilemma. She loved her sister and wanted her to be happy and she was also grateful to and fond of Peter

Townsend. Nevertheless, she made no official pronouncements on her own feelings. That was left to politicians, churchmen and the press, who did not let the subject rest. Nor did the general public, but for different reasons. They flooded the newspapers with letters, making it quite clear that they didn't care whether Peter Townsend was divorced or not: they wanted a romance with a happy ending.

So overwhelming was the divorce as an obstacle to the royal marriage, that two other possible objections were totally ignored. Peter was a commoner and he was sixteen years older than Margaret.

Before the news broke so dramatically in the newspapers, the Queen consulted with the Prime Minister and her advisers. They were all adamant that Peter Townsend should leave Clarence House and some suggested that he should be sent abroad. Perhaps recalling the frustrations and delays in her own romance, the Queen was unwilling to inflict such unhappiness on her sister. With her mother's agreement, she insisted that he should remain at Clarence House and be treated with the fairness and respect he deserved. There were still two years to go before Margaret reached the age of twenty-five and the whole matter could be reconsidered then. However, when the romance was splashed across every newspaper in the country, this compromise was no longer possible.

It had been planned that Peter was to accompany the Queen Mother and Princess Margaret on a visit to South Africa. The visit went ahead, but without him. Instead, he went with the Queen and the Duke of Edinburgh on a routine tour of Ireland. He was then appointed Air Attaché to the British Embassy in Brussels and, by a cruel twist, took up this appointment on the day before Margaret was due to return from South Africa. This virtual exile was not only at the insistence of Winston Churchill, the Prime Minister, but also as a result of Peter's own sense of loyalty to the Crown. It was agreed that the couple should not meet for a year but there was no ban on private letters or telephone calls.

With this separation the matter might have been forgotten, but for the introduction into Parliament of a Bill to amend the Regency Act. The object was to permit the Duke of Edinburgh to act as Regent and guardian of his young son, Charles, should anything happen to the Queen. In itself, this was a sensible safeguard for the monarchy and a recognition of the Duke's sense of responsibility and of his moral right. However, until this amendment, the Regency and guardianship would have passed automatically to Princess Margaret. Inevitably, it was seen in the context of the highly-charged love affair as the first step in enabling Margaret to renounce any possible future claim to the throne and marry Group Captain Townsend.

In spite of the couple's separation, the rumours continued. Newspapers seized on Peter's return to England to take part in a conference in August. They pointed out, some gleefully, some sadly, that he would not be seeing Margaret, who had an official engagement in Scotland at the time. Tall stories surrounded the affair. One newspaper even suggested that Margaret's decision to study religion was an indication that she was so broken-hearted that she was going to take the veil.

Gradually the furore died down. Other events and scandals were more newsworthy and Margaret and Peter had no meetings to revive the dying embers of public interest. For more than a year the story was allowed to lie dormant. Peter acquitted himself well in Brussels and Margaret developed a new skill as a royal ambassadress. One of the major difficulties in Margaret's adult life has been to establish a role that she can make specially her own. As a child, as one of the King's two daughters, she was of as much interest and appeal as her sister. With the births of Prince Charles and Princess Anne, she moved further down the line of succession and, with the Queen's accession to the throne, she found herself at something of a loss in establishing a precise function for herself. Now, overnight, she seemed to change from a giddy young girl to a conscientious and hardworking member of the royal family. In March 1955, she returned triumphant from a tour of the West Indies to universal acclaim.

This was destined to be a fateful year for the Princess. On 21 August she would be twenty-five and, if she still wished to marry Peter Townsend, theoretically the Royal Marriages Act could not prevent her. All she had to do was give the Privy Council twelve months' notice of intent and she would be free to marry him 'except that both Houses of Parliament shall declare their disapprobation thereto'.

Margaret had only just returned from the West Indies when a Sunday newspaper announced in banner headlines that she must now make up her mind. The

Often featured in the press, the attractive and fashion-conscious Princess was the constant companion of her equally photogenic mother, with whom she lived.

affair was definitely front-page news again. The implications were endlessly debated. It was said that, if she married, she would have to renounce all claim to the throne and might face banishment from the royal family. Rival newspapers jockeyed for 'exclusive' interviews with Group Captain Townsend, who found himself besieged in Brussels. Time and time again he pointed out that he could make no comment and that he was unable to make any decision about a marriage. His reticence at this most difficult time earned him the enduring gratitude of the royal family. For a few months the speculation lessened through sheer lack of hard news, but, as the important twenty-fifth birthday approached, the publicity was revived. In July of that year, the press sought the Duke of Windsor's opinion. To the question why Margaret should want to marry a commoner, he replied in words taken from Pascal's *Pensées*, 'The heart has its reasons that reason doesn't know.'

Margaret spent a quiet birthday at Balmoral in Scotland, but the way in which the 'Townsend Affair' occupied the nation can be seen from a letter published in the *Sunday Express* on her birthday. It quoted a horoscope for the Princess, cast in 1930, and stressed the sentence, 'She will marry rather suddenly about twenty-four or twenty-six but as a result of an attachment of long standing.' This was just the sort of fuel to keep the fires of speculation turning. Probably such titbits helped to swell the unprecedented crowds —10,000, according to one account—who turned out to see her go to church the following day.

On 12 October, Peter began a period of leave in London. Simultaneously, Margaret left Balmoral and returned to Clarence House. The stage was set for the final act of this long-drawn-out drama. Hordes of reporters gathered outside the house in Knightsbridge where Peter was staying and dutifully recorded the most minute details of who visited the house, where Peter went and what he bought at the shops. On the evening of 13 October, he called at Clarence House for the eagerly awaited meeting and it was duly recorded that he stayed for one hour, fifty-one minutes. The following weekend, the couple were both house guests at Allanbay Park, Binfield, in Berkshire. This romantic occasion was marked by the first official statement on the affair. The Press Secretary to the Queen was authorized to say that 'no announcement concerning Princess Margaret's personal future is at present contemplated' and, at the same time, he appealed for her privacy to be respected. The fact that

an announcement had been made at all implied the seriousness of the situation and no one was going to worry about the Princess's privacy to the extent of missing a newsworthy story or photograph. The house where the couple were staying was besieged. Reporters and photographers tried to climb walls and break through hedges and teams of policemen patrolled the area. The original plan had been to play down the couple's reunion and allow them the privacy of a friend's home rather than the official stiffness of a royal residence, but it had gone sadly awry.

Princess Margaret drove to morning service in Windsor Chapel on the Sunday and had a deep, forty-minute discussion with her mother after the service. Family opposition to the marriage appeared to be hardening. Meanwhile, in London, it became clear that the Cabinet was about to intervene. A meeting between the Prime Minister, Anthony Eden, and the Queen on 18 October was much longer than usual and this was interpreted as a sign that matters would shortly come to a head. Amidst this debate, Margaret and Peter continued to meet. They dined with friends and attended a party in Knightsbridge, from which the Princess did not return to Clarence House until after one o'clock in the morning. She also kept up her usual round of royal duties.

On 20 October, the Princess and other members of the royal family dined at Lambeth Palace, the London residence of the Archbishop of Canterbury. Was she seeking guidance or pleading her case with the Archbishop? Speculation grew when the Prime Minister and the Archbishop met privately two days later.

Newspapers now declared that there was a rift in the royal family. The Duke of Edinburgh was said to be totally opposed to the marriage and to have influenced the Queen. Some said that she herself was angry. There is no evidence to support either supposition. That there is real affection between the sisters there is no doubt, and it must have been a worrying time for the Queen to watch Margaret torn between her private inclinations and her public responsibilities. However sympathetic she may have felt, she was unable to help and left her sister to make her own decision.

On 26 October, Margaret and Peter met for one-and-a-half hours at Clarence House. It must have been then that she told him of her decision. Shortly after, she spoke to her mother and then had a private interview with the Queen. The following day she had a private audience with the Archbishop of Canterbury and told him also of her decision.

At the weekend, Margaret left London to stay with some friends at Uckfield House in Sussex. The true details of the weekend's events and what was in Margaret's mind will probably never be known. It has been claimed that the decision given to the Queen, the

It is October 1955. The Princess's tear-filled eyes show the pain her decision has caused her.

Queen Mother and the Archbishop of Canterbury earlier in the week was to give up Peter Townsend.

In December 1959, Peter Townsend married Marie-Luce, ending rumours of a reunion with Princess Margaret once and for all. The couple are very happy and live quietly in a converted farmhouse near Paris.

Equally, there is some evidence that she had decided the opposite and intended to marry him and renounce all claims to the throne.

When she left for Uckfield House, she took sixteen trunks in the Buckingham Palace luggage van. Certainly this seems an extraordinarily large number of clothes for a couple of days in the country, even for a Princess. Perhaps she was planning an elopement but she may just as well have been hoping to escape to some hideaway from the oppressive publicity that would follow any announcement that she was giving up the idea or marrying Peter. He was not officially a guest at Uckfield House but was staying with some friends eighteen kilometres (eleven miles) away. Reporters have claimed with pride that they proved he was present during the weekend, but this is hardly surprising. If the Princess intended to give him up it is very likely that she would want to spend one last quiet weekend with him before the public announcement. It seemed much less likely that, if the couple were planning some sort of elopement, they would be indiscreet enough to spend a weekend separated by only a short distance and with such an enormous quantity of luggage.

The luggage van remained at Uckfield until nightfall

when it was driven off to an unknown destination. It returned later with a male passenger who has been identified as Peter Townsend. During the weekend Margaret had two long telephone conversations with her sister and her mother's private secretary visited her twice. The second visit was clearly unexpected and he is reported to have looked worried and to have handed the Princess a private letter from a member of the royal family.

The next day, Margaret returned to London without her sixteen pieces of luggage. Whether the letter was responsible for her return and what it contained, is not known. Perhaps she had always intended to return on Monday or, alternatively, decided that hiding from the press would only give rise to further rumours and speculation. Whether she had made a firm decision the previous week and stuck to it, or experienced a change of heart during the weekend, the die was cast. A statement, approved by both the Queen and the Queen Mother, was issued on 31 October 1955.

'I would like it to be known that I have decided not to marry Group Captain Peter Townsend. I have been aware that, subject to my renouncing my rights of succession, it might have been possible for me to contract a civil marriage. But, mindful of the Church's teaching that Christian marriage is indissoluble, and conscious of my duty to the Commonwealth, I have resolved to put these considerations before any others.

'I have reached this decision entirely alone, and in doing so I have been strengthened by the unfailing support and devotion of Group Captain Townsend. I am deeply grateful for the concern of all those who have constantly prayed for my happiness.

MARGARET'

Reaction to this unequivocal statement was a curious mixture of pomposity and sentimentality. A vicar in Hampshire announced that, had the Princess married, she would have been sinning against God and offending millions of the Queen's subjects. The London newspaper, *The Times*, which had earlier printed a deeply critical editorial stressing that the vast majority of people in the Commonwealth looked to the royal family for a moral example, praised her decision. Others called it courageous and an act of self-sacrifice. Only the *Manchester Guardian* suggested that the whole 'Townsend Affair' had been a storm in a teacup.

Millions of ordinary people expressed their sympathy with the heart-broken Princess, although she was almost universally congratulated for putting her duty above her love. Few things in those dark days can have touched her more than the spontaneous gesture of an unknown woman who stopped a taxi, handed the driver a bunch of flowers and told him to deliver them to Clarence House. It was typical of the warmth with which ordinary people responded to the idea of the Princess's unhappiness.

Early on the morning of 5 November, Peter Townsend was driven to an airport in the country and from there he flew to Brussels. Newspapers reported that Margaret remained at Clarence House, answering letters at a desk which no longer held Peter's silver-framed photograph. Later he went on a world tour—supposedly to 'forget'—and to make a documentary film of his travels.

Even then the topic was not allowed to rest. The affair, at least as far as the press was concerned, dragged on until 1959. The lovers remained in touch as they had throughout the period of enforced separation. But news of a mere telephone call was enough to stir up speculation again. The princess was said countless times to be seeking permission to marry Peter. His photograph was spotted by her bedside when she was on a visit to Canada. When papers were stolen from his car in Paris, it was, predictably, claimed that they included 'personal letters from the Princess'. At one point it was even confidently stated that they were going to become Roman Catholics in order to marry, although the logic of this twisted piece of theology is obscure.

In 1958 they did meet again. Instantly they were headline news and a royal wedding was in many minds. Peter Townsend could bear the rumours no longer and issued a statement: 'There are no grounds whatever for supposing that my seeing Princess Margaret in any way alters the situation declared in the Princess's statement in the autumn of 1955.' The Princess never went back on her statement and, indeed, it is difficult to see how she could. She had met Peter, written to him and spoken to him on the telephone, but none of this implies that she had second thoughts about her decision not to marry him.

In December 1959, Peter Townsend married Marie-Luce Jamagne in Paris and the rumours at last died down. Barely five months later, the Princess herself was married. A nation which had shared intimately in her earlier love now wished her the happiness for which she had waited.

94

Prince Edward of Kent
&
Katharine Worsley

Edward and Katharine

orn in 1935, Prince Edward, known to his family as Eddie, was the eldest of the Duke and Duchess of Kent's three children. Deeply in love with each other, the Duke and Duchess were thrilled with their family and lavished attention on their children. The second child, Alexandra, was born fourteen months after her brother and they have remained especially close to each other ever since. When they were little they delighted in the stimulating and loving atmosphere which provided them with the security growing children need.

Not long after the birth of their daughter, the Duke and Duchess moved from London's fashionable Belgravia, where the royal children could not easily be kept out of the public eye, to a larger and more comfortable house, Coppins, in Buckinghamshire. Only thirty-two kilometres (twenty miles) from the heart of London, their new home was sufficiently remote and away from the public gaze to please the Kents, who believed very strongly that their children should be brought up to be as 'ordinary' as possible.

From the children's earliest years, pocket money was restricted and no amount of pleading by them could persuade their parents to add a penny to it. While they were still too young for formal education, they learned a good deal simply from living in with their parents. Marina's background was cosmopolitan in the extreme, connected as she was by birth to almost all the royal houses of Europe, and there was a constant flow of foreign relatives through the house which rang with Marina's gay, unrestrained chatter in a variety of languages.

Nothing seemed to mar their happiness because, as far as possible, nothing was allowed to do so. Even World War II seemed incapable of harming them. But it did. Shortly after the birth of Prince Michael in 1942, just when it seemed that the family was even happier than ever before, because of the arrival of the new baby, the plane carrying the Duke on a wartime mission to Iceland crashed, killing him instantly.

Apart from their private sorrow at the loss of a loving and much-loved husband and father, the family had practical difficulties to face. The Duchess had no income apart from an Air Commodore's widow's pension and any funds which could be raised by selling the Duke's private collection of antiques. Most of the estate was in trust for Eddie, now the new Duke and seventh in line of succession to the throne. The Duchess set about bringing up her children on a strict budget and it is, perhaps, this which has given the Kents their air of 'ordinariness' which so appeals to the British people. The Duchess raised her children with imagination and courage and watched with pride as they matured. She often remarked how much Eddie reminded her of her husband, for he had not only inherited his father's good looks, but also his urbanity, tact and relaxed manner.

In the mid 1950s, Eddie was one of the officers in the regiment of the Royal Scots Greys at Catterick Camp in Yorkshire, invited to a dance at Hovingham Hall, near York. As his host's lovely daughter, Katharine Worsley, showed him around the old Manor House, he found it difficult to take his eyes off her. With his passionate Romanov blood, inherited from his mother, he fell in love there and then.

he Worsley family have been the 'local gentry' in Hovingham since the reign of the first Elizabeth. One branch of the family took sides with Oliver Cromwell, the Lord Protector who, during the Civil War, stabled his horse in the cathedral in York, known as York Minster, as a gesture against its 'popish' Gothic interior. In spite of Cromwell and his republicanism, the monarchy survived and even flourished, and, ironically, a descendant of one of his staunchest followers was to marry into the royal family in the great church where he had once kept his horse over three hundred years before.

Katharine was the only daughter of Sir William Worsley, the fourth Baronet and former Lord Lieutenant of the North Riding of Yorkshire. She had led a very ordinary life: not surprisingly, since she had four brothers, she was a tomboy and one of her greatest pleasures was entering local riding competitions. She was well-known in Hovingham and universally liked, having, as the locals say, 'no edge'—meaning that she never stood on ceremony and was polite to everyone.

As she grew older, she lost her childish plumpness and became a vivacious, slim, engaging blonde with a determination to work for her living. Typically of a Yorkshire woman, 'Miss Kate' had never been afraid of hard work and so she was undaunted by the demands of being a helper at St Stephen's Orphanage in York. Always understaffed, St Stephen's expected helpers to undertake many of the least agreeable tasks in caring for children. Mrs Elsie Cobb, the matron, remembers Katharine's unstinting efforts and her willingness to stay later than her set hours so that she

could read or sing to the children.

There are some striking similarities between the young Katharine Worsley and her contemporary, Princess Alexandra. Both were plump tomboys as children and later matured into attractive and elegant young women with considerable flair and chic in matters of fashion. Both are known for their perfect manners and ability to put others at their ease. Both worked unstintingly with children, giving up many hours of their time. Perhaps it was seeing instinctively in Katharine the valued qualities so familiar in his sister, that made the Duke recognize her worth immediately.

The romance became one of the closest guarded of modern times. If they were both invited to dinner, for example, Katharine would arrive first with an escort and the Duke would come later.

Desperately in love, Eddie wanted her to meet his family, especially his mother, but also his sister and

The Worsleys are a close and loving family and Kate is always especially pleased to see her young nephews and nieces. It is difficult to believe that this elegant young woman of 1961 was ever a tomboy but her brothers Marcus, Oliver and John (left to right) saw to that.

his brother, Prince Michael. A weekend at Coppins was arranged and, as Eddie drove Katharine up the drive, he casually mentioned that Aunt Elizabeth would be there. Only when Katharine stepped through the French windows did the significance of the name sink in. There, taking tea, with her unmistakable charm, was HRH Queen Elizabeth, the Queen Mother. For a few minutes Katharine felt awkward, for it is one thing to have a baronet for a father but quite another to have the Queen Mother as a prospective aunt. As always, however, 'Aunt Elizabeth' showed her only warmth and kindness, and, as for the rest of the family, how could they fail to take to this

The Duchess of Kent warmly welcomed the charming and pretty girl her son had chosen for his wife. The engagement was announced on 8 March 1961.

fresh-faced and charming girl?

Although the Duchess of Kent approved whole-heartedly of her son's choice, she would not allow a whirlwind marriage. No one knew better than she what it was to be head over heels in love but she insisted that they spent time apart to ensure that they really were meant for each other. Although they dreaded the prospect, the young lovers saw the wisdom in this. They spent the next four years apart, Katharine as an assistant in a jewellery store in Vancouver, Canada, and Eddie abroad with his regiment. They corresponded endlessly, dreaming of meeting again and of marriage.

On 8 March 1961, the Duchess of Kent announced her son's engagement, 'to which the Queen has gladly given her consent'. They had just three months to make the wedding arrangements. This was not a simple matter: the ceremony was not to be a straight-forward repetition of other royal weddings in West-minster Abbey, because Kate wanted very much to be married in York Minster. It is, perhaps, a measure of the Queen's delight at the match and her personal affection for Kate that she agreed to travel, together with members of the British and other European royal families, to York, incidentally giving the ancient and beautiful city another cause for pride.

On Marina's advice—and who better to give it on matters of fashion than she—Katharine went to the designer John Cavanagh for her dress. He worked for Captain Edward Molyneux, who had made Princess Marina's own beautiful wedding dress in 1934. Five

A sparkling guest at gala occasions, the Duchess's warmth and charm have won her immense popularity.

designs were shortlisted and it was essential that the one chosen should both flatter the bride and not be overwhelmed by the soaring splendour of the Minster's nave, where the procession would take place. The final choice suited the Duchess-to-be to perfection. The train, four and a half metres (fifteen feet) long, seemed unwieldy in the confined space of the fitting room but Cavanagh explained that a television camera perched high up a stone column in the nave would scale it down perfectly.

A royal bride has one more problem on her wedding day than an ordinary girl. As she leaves on the arm of her new husband, she must curtsey to the Queen. This seemed, at first, an impossibility for Katharine, with four and a half metres of white gauze silk attached at head and waist. But she worked out a method of stepping back into its folds gracefully and after practising by kneeling on stacks of telephone directories, she managed it perfectly.

*T*he confined area round York Minster was thronged with people in the early hours of 8 June, and word passed quickly through the ancient streets that the royal train had arrived. The only other royal wedding to take place within the Minster walls had been in 1328 when King Edward III married Philippa of Hainault. Katharine Worsley knew that she was making history in her own, quietly determined way that day.

The guests included Earl Mountbatten and his two daughters, the Earl of Harewood, Noel Coward, the playwright, and other people who were famous in the theatre and film world and, of course, Mrs Elsie Cobb, matron of St Stephen's. Apart from members of the British royal family, the distinguished guest list included Norwegian, Greek, Dutch, Yugoslavian, Prussian and Danish royalty.

Everyone watching remarked how lovely Princess Margaret looked in her fashionable cool blue duster coat, its soft lines concealing the fact that she was expecting her first child. The Queen Mother wore her favourite shade of blue, and one of her famous feathery hats framed the bonniest of smiles. The Queen, dressed in a lilac silk ensemble, was accompanied by the Duke of Edinburgh and the Prince of Wales. The groom's family blazed forth. Princess Marina wore gold-embroidered champagne coloured organza with a superb fluffy hat tilted with characteristic chic to one side. Princess Alexandra, smiling delightedly, wore a glorious shade of pink. The groom was in his regiment's old ceremonial uniform of

scarlet and blue, complete with sword. Special permission had to be obtained from the War Office for this somewhat archaic dress uniform to be worn on this occasion.

The bride entered the Minster to the sound of

Like her mother-in-law, the Duchess of Kent has become famous for her elegance, adapting current fashions to suit her own style and taste.

trumpet fanfares and seemed to glide in on the arm of her father. Among her eight bridesmaids were Princess Anne and two girls of the Worsley family. There was another young Worsley among the three page boys. After the ceremony, the slow and elegant curtsey worked beautifully, and the Queen and Queen Mother, no doubt knowing the problems it had entailed, smiled their blessings warmly. As the couple came out into the sunshine under the crossed swords of soldiers from the Duke's regiment, cheers rang round the city.

Two thousand guests thronged the grounds of Hovingham Hall that evening for the wedding reception, at which the bride and groom cut the cake with the Duke's ceremonial sword.

Edward and Katharine

In a cloud of confetti thrown by royal hands, the couple made their way to an RAF station nearby to board a Heron of the Queen's Flight to take them on the first part of their honeymoon. They stayed first at the Queen Mother's residence on the Balmoral estate and then went on to Spain.

It was quite obvious that Katharine's great love of children meant a happy family life, in spite of the pressures of being an army wife. George, Earl of St Andrews, was born a year after their marriage, Lady Helen in 1964 and Lord Nicholas in 1970. Army wives remember the Duchess of Kent cheerfully pushing her two youngest in a supermarket trolley while she went shopping in Hong Kong. If army wives have a reputation for being stuffy abroad, this was one who was out of a different mould.

In due course the Duke left the army and took a job in Whitehall and, in 1968, on the death of his mother, he inherited the much loved country home, Coppins.

The Duke and Duchess of Kent frequently represent the Queen at official functions and perform their royal duties with unfailing good humour and élan.

Meanwhile the royal round continued: the Kents followed the tradition established by Princess Marina of officiating at the prizegiving at the Wimbledon Tennis Tournament each year, as well as fulfilling many other engagements. The Duchess's name has become a by-word for sympathy and good humour, so it was all the more tragic when her 'Jubilee baby' miscarried. For a time afterwards she was unwell but, as soon as possible, she once more undertook the arduous responsibilities of helping the Queen as a royal ambassadress.

And so this generation of the Kents have added to the special legacy of love and popularity which they have inherited through so many of their illustrious ancestors.

Princess Margaret
&
Antony Armstrong-Jones

To be separated for ever from the man she loves, for whatever reason, is inexpressibly painful for any woman, and the blaze of publicity which surrounded Princess Margaret's relationship with Group Captain Peter Townsend can only have increased her suffering and distress. It was, therefore, all the more delightful that, when her engagement to Antony Armstrong-Jones was announced on 26 February 1960, it came as quite a surprise to the press and the public. The romance, which had blossomed over the previous two years, had remained more or less secret because, whenever the couple had appeared together in public, it was assumed that Tony was there in his professional capacity as a photographer. In addition, although the days were long past when suitable marriages for Princesses were made, not in heaven but at the Palace, Tony did not come from the background traditionally associated with royal husbands.

Tony's father was a Welsh barrister, Ronald Owen Lloyd Armstrong-Jones and his mother, who had divorced his father, was married to the Earl of Rosse. His sister was the Countess de Vesci and his half-brother Lord Oxmantown. This meant that Tony was what Burke's Peerage, the book describing the British aristocracy and its ranks—would call an 'untitled aristocrat'—in other words, a commoner. He was educated at Eton and Cambridge and had been a keen rower until the age of fifteen, when he developed polio, which left him with a permanently wasted left leg. Even so, he was still known as the 'pocket Tarzan' among his friends. It was during the period of enforced inactivity caused by his illness that he developed an interest in photography, which eventually dominated his years at Cambridge and ousted the subject he had at first chosen for his degree: architecture. Later, he brought about a minor revolution in fashion photography, for it was he who first had the idea of posing models against incongruous settings, such as rubbish bins.

He had a house in a crumbling Georgian terrace in Pimlico, near London's Victoria Station, and had made it into his studio. Princess Margaret often escaped there and enjoyed cooking bacon and eggs for the two of them in the small kitchen. Both she and Tony shared a love of the unconventional, sometimes to a quite extreme extent. They also had a mutual love of the arts and many other tastes in common.

Previous page Margaret and Tony together in the days of love. Their happiness was unmistakable.

The Queen, who had been deeply sympathetic to her sister throughout the 'Townsend Affair', was delighted to see the gradual regrowth of Margaret's warmth, spontaneity and *joie de vivre* as she fell in love and was loved in return. Also, she personally liked her future brother-in-law with whom she shared a number of interests and whose sense of humour was very like her own. Although royal marriages usually follow a prolonged period of courtship, the Queen, clearly remembering the agony of the long-drawn-out romance with Peter, made no suggestion that the couple should wait.

English folk-lore is very definite about some things and old wives say that it is unlucky to get married on a Friday or in May. Typically, Margaret defied tradition and did both: the wedding was on Friday, 6 May 1960. Contrary to expectation, it was not an official State occasion. The spectre of divorce once again raised its head because the bridegroom's parents had both remarried. Indeed, Margaret had a choice of three mothers-in-law, one of whom was only a year or so older than she. The wedding invitations had been issued by the Lord Chamberlain, on behalf of the Queen Mother, not the Queen. The reception after the ceremony was for one hundred and twenty guests and was not a gathering of official dignitaries.

Protocol had also caused problems over the choice of best man. Tony had originally chosen a close friend, Jeremy Fry, but a conviction for a homosexual offence eight years previously precluded him from taking such a central role in a royal wedding. Dr Roger Gilliat was selected instead, although he himself admitted that he was not one of Tony's closest friends. By coincidence, his father, Sir William Gilliat, had supervised the births of Princess Anne and Prince Charles.

These problems were so out of keeping with the usual procedures for the marriage of a British Princess that many members of the royal houses of Europe refused invitations to the wedding. However, the guest list did include the French writer, Jean Cocteau, René, Princess Margaret's hairdresser, Jacqueline Chan, a former girlfriend of the bridegroom, Mrs Peabody, who did his housework and Mrs Mona Playfair, his first photographic model who had flown from Australia especially for the occasion.

The British public, however, cared little for the wrangles over protocol. A crowd of 40,000 had been massing for two or three days and, carefully warned by the police not to bring stools or seats in case of accidents, stood waiting under the banners and

Radiantly happy, Margaret shows Tony one of the many telegrams of congratulations and good wishes which followed the announcement of their engagement in 1960.

flowers that lined the route. It was a warm, sunny day and it was a royal wedding, the first to be broadcast live on television. If, in the past, there had been criticism of the Princess, on 'her day' everyone was wishing her well.

Inside the Abbey, two thousand guests had assembled. Prince Charles wore a kilt of Royal Stuart tartan. The Duchess of Kent was in lemon yellow, Princess Alexandra in aquamarine, the Queen Mother in gold with sable trimmings and the Queen, fully recovered from the recent birth of Prince Andrew, looked radiant in a turquoise outfit with a hat of roses in two shades, set on a net base. Her dress, like those of the other royal ladies, was long, as custom decreed when a close member of the family married. (This custom was discarded at Princess Anne's wedding.)

The Princess rode to the Abbey in the Glass Coach, accompanied by Prince Philip. As she alighted, a fanfare of sixteen trumpets, specially composed by Sir Arthur Bliss, 'the Master of the Queen's Musick', rang out and the waiting onlookers could see the bridal gown for the first time. It was a stunningly simple design. The dress had a close-fitting bodice, a V-neckline, tight sleeves and waist, and a short, unobtrusive train. The only ornament was the organza piping down the neckline and the panels of the skirt, and around the hem. A single layer of plain tulle, again edged with organza, was set round her upswept hair and diamond tiara. She carried a bouquet of mixed orchids, stephanotis and myrtle. The myrtle, in the tradition of royal brides, was picked from Queen Victoria's bush at Osborne. Margaret had never looked so beautiful.

Because Margaret was without a father, Prince Philip was to give her away. He smiled and whispered to her as, holding nervously on to his arm, she began the long walk to the altar. Eight small bridesmaids, including Princess Anne, followed, dressed in scaled-down replicas of 'Papa's dress', Margaret's first evening dress which had been a particular favourite of her father, George VI. Once they had completed the long and rather terrifying procession over the blue carpet stretched along the sixty-metre (two-hundred-foot) aisle, the solemnity of the familiar service took over. The Dean of Westminster and the Archbishop of Canterbury conducted the ceremony and the bride was married with a ring made from the same nugget of Welsh gold as the Queen's had been. Finally, after a deep bow and curtsey to their Sovereign, Mr and Mrs Armstrong-Jones made their way, hand-in-hand, down the centre aisle and out into the sunshine. The Abbey bells rang out as the wedding party set off back down the Mall, the long, wide avenue leading to Buckingham Palace.

After photographs had been taken in the throne room, the newly-weds stood on the balcony of Buckingham Palace and waved to the jubilant crowd. At the reception, Prince Philip toasted the couple and then the 68-kilogram (150-pound) cake, made to a secret recipe, was cut.

Later, Margaret, now dressed in sunshine yellow, drove with Tony in a Rolls Royce to the waiting royal yacht *Britannia*. (The car had to be resprayed afterwards as an enthusiastic well-wisher had scratched a heart and the couple's initials in the paintwork.) Their choice of the West Indies for a honeymoon was a popular one. The West Indians loved Princess Margaret, or the 'dolly Princess' as they fondly called her, and they were all set to give the couple a 'calypso honeymoon' that they would never forget.

For Tony it may have been a moment for reflection as he braved the inquisitive crowds. From now on his life must change. He must learn to accept second place on occasions and, if necessary, sacrifice some of his friends and habits. He had, too, to learn to live a life hemmed in by protocol, where privacy would be rare. But the Queen Mother is reported to have said that they were made for each other and, as they sat on the deck in the sunshine, these doubts were easy to forget and it was simple to imagine that the future would always be so sunny.

The six-week Caribbean honeymoon was idyllic. Best of all, for some of the time they managed to remain isolated from the prying eyes of press cameras. Margaret said, 'It was so wonderful for us both just to lie on those deserted beaches, without a soul in sight . . . we would have gladly lived in a little grass hut.' However, they didn't escape the hounding of reporters completely. One, more enterprising and less scrupulous than the rest, broke into the Princess's dressing room to rummage through her clothes and scooped the story that her underwear was made of crêpe de chine. Such attentions amused and angered Margaret by turns but she had expected them. Tony had not and found them rather more difficult to cope with.

The small apartment in Kensington Palace in London, which was the Armstrong-Jones's first home, was a present from the Queen. The royal apartments at Number 10, which Margaret delightedly called 'a doll's house', were on the first floor, sandwiched between the staff quarters on the ground floor and second floor. Very much in love, Margaret and Tony greatly enjoyed the challenge of redesigning their first home, choosing colour schemes and occasionally turning their own hands to decorating.

They soon stamped their individual styles on the place. Margaret's bedroom was a paradise of pink filled with bowls of roses. Tony's dressing room was a showplace for his work and that of his friends, with framed photographs and large, modern paintings on the walls. The drawing room was white-painted and conservatively furnished. There were touches typical of Margaret's hand, such as a singing bird in a gilded cage on the piano, next to a photograph of her mother, and a bust of George VI on the desk next to a plain, carved, wooden crucifix. There were bright signs of Tony's personality, too: a handmade red and black rug in front of the fire and water colours and pastels on the walls. As an ever-present reminder of the royal background, there were three telephones, two of them direct lines to Clarence House and Buckingham Palace.

Much as they loved their 'doll's house', it wasn't big enough for children and when the larger Number 1A became vacant, they moved. The royal apartment had twenty rooms and Tony was able to have a workroom and a darkroom. There was also a large playroom for

The colour and pageantry made the wedding magical.
Margaret was a fairy-tale bride. As she married the man
she loved the whole nation wished her well.

their children and a dingy, little downstairs room was converted into a small cinema with dramatic red walls and a black carpet.

In spite of the pleasures of organizing their home and the new-found joys of parenthood, when their son and daughter were born in 1961 and 1964 respectively, all was not well in the Armstrong-Jones household. Indeed, there had been problems for some time. Even before their wedding, Margaret and Tony had had major disagreements. Most engaged couples do quarrel a little under the strain of pre-wedding nerves, but for these two, the underlying difficulties were fundamental and would end by undermining their whole way of life.

When he married the beautiful and high-spirited Margaret, with whom he had so much in common, Tony hoped, in the words of the Hollywood cliché, 'to take her away from all this'. 'All this', in their case, was the stultifying royal round. He felt that Margaret was temperamentally unsuited to the life of a British Princess and one of his least critical comments about it was that it was 'not much fun at all'. But, despite her bohemianism, her somewhat wild ways, her furious moods, Tony had overlooked one essential side of his wife's character—the very royalness he hoped to help her escape from. Whatever else she might have, Margaret was first and foremost a Princess and she rarely forgot it. Tony, apparently, had not wanted their wedding to take place in Westminster Abbey, although it seems highly unrealistic of him to imagine the Queen's sister marrying quietly and obscurely. Margaret, on the other hand, revelled in the elegance and ceremonial of the occasion. After all, most brides enjoy being the 'star' on their wedding day.

Opinions vary about how Tony got on with his 'in-laws'—the Queen Mother, the Queen, Prince Philip and other members of that most formidable of families into which to marry. His relationship with them now, in spite of the past difficulties in his marriage, suggests that both the Queen and Queen Mother liked him a great deal then. Prince Philip was reported to be openly hostile, however, and is credited with the comment, 'I have my doubts about any man whose best friends are male ballet dancers.'

Problems over money and budgeting are often the cause of quarrels and difficulties in ordinary marriages but no one expects them to occur for a Princess and her husband. Both Margaret and Tony loved to entertain, both officially and unofficially. They delighted in sparkling, lively and witty company although, some-times, their unroyal guests, who included pop stars, ballet dancers, actors and actresses, caused such a noise in the early hours of the morning that the police were called out by irate neighbours. But entertaining, especially on the scale that Margaret liked to do it, costs a great deal of money. Tony already had something of a reputation for holding firmly on to the purse strings and Margaret's truly royal extravagance angered him. Not only was he annoyed with his wife, but also with the servants for running up such large household bills. Within a relatively short space of time, three butlers handed in their notice and other servants followed. Margaret was beside herself with humiliation and fury. Her father had been the King, her sister was the Queen and here was her own husband, asking her to account for every penny. The disagreements over money grew worse and became an unpleasant and recurring theme in their life together.

By the time their son was born, eighteen months after the wedding, Tony had accepted a title and had become the Earl of Snowdon and Keeper of the Keys of Caernarvon Castle. The Queen, who very much wanted to please him in this highly-charged matter, had consulted him about exactly what title would be fitting for him as her brother-in-law, yet not offensive to his democratic views. It was reported that Margaret was not pleased and had wanted her husband to be a Duke, equal in rank to her sister's husband, although Philip had also been granted the title, Prince, in 1957.

A title for Tony, however, resulted in public and private confusion. To begin with, he accompanied his wife on the round of official royal duties. In the early 1960s they made a number of successful tours in Britain and abroad. But Tony loved his profession as a designer and photographer and it became increasingly clear that, although he dutifully appeared at his wife's side at official functions, he did so uneasily and grudgingly. He eventually did take 'official' jobs—as an unpaid consultant at the Design Centre in London and as designer of, among other things, a revolutionary new invalid chair and an aviary in London Zoo. This last task brought him a great deal of criticism from both press and public. The newspaper, *Daily Express*, said that he 'must now be ranked as one of the leading bird cage designers in the country. Not an over-crowded profession.' Finally, with the Queen's approval, he took a full-time position with the *Sunday Times* newspaper as Artistic Adviser to the paper's new colour supplement. This threw Fleet Street into

By 1972, their marriage was already breaking down and, although Tony accompanied his wife on formal occasions, they appeared together less and less frequently.

intelligent, irreverent people who had been her husband's friends before their marriage.

She was deeply, passionately, in love with Tony but the love became corroded by jealousy and possessiveness. Married life became an emotional obstacle race as Margaret caused scenes over real or imagined slights. At a ball in aid of the Dockland Settlement charity, she and Tony naturally had a number of different dancing partners but Margaret noticed that he had been dancing with the same attractive young woman for much of the evening. Smiling sweetly, she asked the girl if she were enjoying the dance. 'Yes, ma'am, very much,' replied the unfortunate guest. 'Then run along home, you've had enough for one night,' snapped the Princess, narrowing her brilliant blue eyes in a way which signalled the beginning of one of her moods. Scenes and marital rows became more and more public and it grew clear that Margaret's jealousy was reaching an extreme pitch.

Marriage intensified the fundamental problem of Margaret's adult life. Her inclination was to be a young woman of the moment, part of the social revolution taking place in the 'swinging Sixties', but her background, upbringing and training all emphasized the need for convention, discretion and circumspection. Whether she liked it or not, she was constantly in the public eye and open to the severest criticism. Furthermore, this criticism was not simply limited to her, but reflected on the entire royal family. She began to wear trendy clothes, even at the most sober functions. The fashions acceptable for seventeen-year-olds were not so appropriate, at least in the eyes of the press and the public, for a Princess in her mid-thirties. An outfit she wore on one occasion for inspecting the troops was basically a midi-length skirt, a mini fur jacket and a huge Mickey Mouse watch!

Then there was what the press came to call the 'Meg and Tony show', their contribution to a royal tour of the United States. Opinions varied about its success, although the Americans seemed charmed by her and a little bewildered by him. But there were hitches, tantrums and unpunctuality. The trip cost Britain a great deal of money and unfortunately coincided with a rising tide of general criticism about the expense to the country of the royal family. Even so, few people queried the cost of the Queen's tours and the Snowdons were probably singled out for such criticism largely because it was becoming fashionable to snipe at them.

It seemed particularly appropriate that, during their American tour, they visited the other 'black sheep' of the family, the Duke and Duchess of Windsor, at the

paroxysms of sour-grape fury—except, of course, the *Sunday Times* Group which had the Queen's brother-in-law on its staff. It is hard to see what else Tony, who was criticized whether he worked or not, could have done. There is no doubt that, with his talent and experience, he could well have achieved the same post without any royal connections.

The dilemma for Margaret became more acute and she found it harder to handle. On the one hand she delighted in a life which, by royal standards, was very unconventional, untrammelled by regulations and protocol. On the other, she wasn't able to forget that she was a royal, nor did she want to. She would, on occasion, remind people that she was a Princess. She insisted on being treated with the courtesy traditionally expected by a member of the royal family. Yet, at the same time, she gathered round her the same bright,

Waldorf Hotel in New York. To Margaret, of course, the Duke was the uncle she had always liked best, who had played games with her and spoilt her as a child, so, naturally, she wanted her husband to meet him.

The Snowdons returned to a cool reception in Britain. Their popularity was on the wane. They were both seen as frivolous, irresponsible and spoilt. Margaret's health began to suffer and this, in turn, affected her looks. Single, spoilt but beautiful, she had been popular and forgivable, but a puffy-faced and matronly Margaret, clinging on to her youth in an undignified manner, was not.

The Snowdons were seen together less and less frequently and in the late 1960s British newspapers began to hint at what American and continental newspapers had been saying for a long time—that the marriage was breaking up and divorce was in the air. At this time, Tony was very friendly with Lady Jacqueline Rufus Isaacs and, in 1970, she misguidedly visited him when he was in hospital for a short stay. It may be that Margaret didn't visit him at all or, which is more likely, that her concern was less newsworthy than Lady Jacqueline's. At about the same time, Margaret met the 'intriguing young gypsy', the upper-class drop-out, Roddy Llewellyn, during a weekend stay at the country house of a friend. As their friendship grew, so did press speculation about the nature of their relationship. An impertinent and salacious article in the British satirical magazine *Private Eye* was followed by increasingly unsavoury stories in the rest of the press.

Meanwhile, the public hardly ever saw Margaret carrying out any official duties. In spite of specialist medical help, she found it hard to control her moods. There was no guarantee that she would actually arrive at a function at all, let alone be punctual, gracious and interested. Other royal ladies, such as Princess Alexandra and the Duchess of Kent, undertook more duties to avoid embarrassment but even traditionally pro-royalist publications, such as women's magazines, began to criticize the Princess and accuse her of being idle.

She seemed to be living almost permanently in the Caribbean, on the island of Mustique. A plot of land on the island had, ironically, been a wedding present from a friend and a villa had been built there. Often,

Rumours that the Queen disliked her brother-in-law were quite unfounded. She enjoyed his company and included him in all kinds of family parties and visits.

Fun-loving Roddy Llewellyn is 17 years Margaret's junior. Their friendship was kept private for several years before publicized by the popular press.

Margaret took a party of friends, or sometimes Roddy alone. Every effort was made to keep journalists off the island but, inevitably, one slipped through the net. In February 1976, the British Sunday newspaper, *News of the World*, published a story and pictures showing Margaret and Roddy, in comfortable holiday shabbiness, taking a lunchtime drink together. The photograph was splashed across every front page, even in Britain. It was only a matter of time before the Snowdon marriage was officially over; the pretence could no longer be kept up.

Margaret had already spoken to her family about the impending collapse of her marriage and the Queen, hoping for a reconciliation, had urged delay. Patching up the marriage would be the happiest solution for everyone but, when that clearly became an impossibility, with characteristic realism, she turned to a separation agreement. The failure of a marriage is always emotional and distressing and the publicity surrounding this one only made it more unbearable. The legal and financial arrangements were made surprisingly quickly. Margaret was given custody of the children and Tony moved to a house in central London. It has been claimed that Margaret accused her sister of taking Tony's side but, in fact, the Queen demonstrated impressive understanding of the difficulties and immense kindness and concern. She herself was a personal friend of Tony's and, once the rift was recognized as irreversible, she wanted to smooth the path for both him and her sister. She quietly included Tony among the guests invited to family celebrations, such as her own birthday party. The royal family's realistic and low-key approach caused the story to lose its fire in the newspapers.

After the public announcement of the separation on 19 March 1976, Margaret seemed to disappear from public view. When she emerged a few months later, she was slimmer, more relaxed and composed and was soon busy again with the royal round. After all the unkind comments in the past few years, it must have been a pleasant surprise to hear one young man in the crowd at Royal Ascot call out, 'You're looking great, Maggie!'

To a certain extent, the constitutional side of the divorce had been made easier by a precedent set in 1967, when the Queen's cousin, the Earl of Harewood was divorced. Nevertheless, Margaret must have been embarrassed and hurt when reporters quoted the statement she had made in 1955 to announce her decision not to marry Group Captain Townsend: '. . . mindful of the Church's teaching that Christian marriage is indissoluble, and conscious of my duty to the Commonwealth . . .'

Little appears in the newspapers today, linking Margaret and her young friend, Roddy. For a while, many thought that, after the divorce in 1978, she might once again try to battle against tradition and marry him. But, chastened by her experiences and more knowledgeable, perhaps, about her own emotions, she has learned to separate her public and private lives successfully and discreetly.

A little while after the divorce, Tony married his research assistant, Lucy Lindsay-Hogg, herself a divorcée. It is hard to imagine anyone less like Margaret. The new Countess is shy, introverted and not very fond of parties and socializing. The couple have a baby daughter and seem very happy. Tony retains a deep love and concern for the children of his first marriage, David and Sarah, often visiting them and taking them out.

As for the Princess, she has acquired a new com-

posure and self-awareness. In this calmer frame of mind, now that the shouting has all died down, she must appreciate the real sympathy and love of her mother and sister. She often chooses to spend the weekend with her children and the Queen Mother.

Margaret and Tony

Once, when quite young, she compared herself to her sister: 'Lilibet is so serious and dutiful that they expect me to be as wicked as hell.' Perhaps she has now grown out of trying to live up to 'their' expectations and perhaps her luck has, at last, turned.

Tony and his second wife, Lucy, proudly show off their newly-christened daughter, Frances, in October 1979. They were joined by Frances' half-brother and half-sister, David, Viscount Linley, and Lady Sarah Armstrong-Jones, and her grandmother, the Countess of Rosse.

114

Princess Alexandra of Kent
&
Angus Ogilvy

The birth of Alexandra on Christmas Day 1936 was a cheerful and heartening event for the royal family and for the nation, still dazed by the shock of the Abdication earlier in the same month. Eighth in line of succession to the throne, she was born into one of the happiest and most unassuming of modern royal families. Her parents, the Duke and Duchess of Kent, had already secured the affection of the nation and the new baby, christened Alexandra Helen Elizabeth Olga Christabel, made a perfect companion for her brother Eddie, who was only fourteen months her senior.

The world Alexandra knew as a toddler was to change rapidly and tragically but, for a brief time, she delighted in the warm family atmosphere of a loving

Previous page Angus Ogilvy and Princess Alexandra were married on 24 April 1963.

Below The Ogilvies and Kents celebrate the couple's engagement amid the chill Scottish winter.

home. Shortly after her birth, the Kents moved from their grace-and-favour residence in London's Belgravia to Coppins, in Buckinghamshire. The Duchess, remembering the happy freedom of her childhood, instructed the children's new nanny, Miss Ethel Wright, not to make a fuss of the children but to teach them to do what they were told.

Both the Duke and Duchess wanted their son and daughter to lead lives as normal and ordinary as possible. Their pocket money was strictly limited and the village shop had strict instructions not to take pity on the woeful Kent children who both had a 'sweet tooth'. As they passed out of their nursery days, they came under the charge of a governess, Miss Peebles. Known to them as 'Bambi', she was tremendously popular and stayed with the family until they outgrew the need for her. She was so successful with the little Kents that she later went on to teach the young Prince Charles and Princess Anne.

The little Alexandra appreciated the warmth and liveliness of her home life and gave it a child's greatest

praise when she said, 'I like it even when it rains.' But the peace and security of that life, which even the outbreak of World War II couldn't shatter, was destroyed by the untimely death of her father in 1942. The children were all very young—Prince Michael just a tiny baby—but Alexandra recalls the appalling moment when her mother, totally distraught, rushed into the nursery and broke the news to them. They couldn't believe that their beloved father wasn't coming back, but as the days lengthened into weeks without him and their mother's tears were still just below the surface, it hit them hard that it was indeed true. If 'sweet money' had been a strain on the Kent finances, they now faced a harsher reality. The Duchess had only a small income and most of the Coppins estate was in trust for the new Duke, little Eddie, now seventh in line of succession to the throne, and whose future must, of necessity, come before Alexandra's.

Yet the Duchess was to prove herself a superb manager and an almost one-woman finishing school for her daughter. A thoroughly modern mother, Marina decided to send her daughter to school. This seems unsurprising today, when the heir to the throne spent part of his school days in Australia and his brother went to school in the wilds of Canada, but Alexandra was the first royal girl to go to a boarding school. Princess Marina visited many schools and finally decided on Heathfield School, near Ascot. The Princess arrived there in her ready-made uniform and soon fitted in with school routine. Everyone, including the young Princess, was expected to attend all lessons, play games and do a variety of chores: Alexandra was never let off any duties because she might dislike them. She appeared in her apron with her sleeves rolled up and quipped, 'I'm the new char. I'm Mrs Kent.' Already her charm and amiable nature were apparent and she made friends easily. No restrictions were placed upon whom she could choose as friends and Princess Marina was delighted that her daughter was mixing with girls of her own age.

As she was so close to her elder brother, it was almost inevitable that Alexandra should be something of a tomboy. Like many of the royal family, she rode well and entered a number of local sporting events. At home in the holidays, like her cousin Princess Anne later, she cared for and groomed her horses as well as riding them. As a teenager she ran to puppy fat and remained boyish. She might well have been the despair of her mother, whose natural chic had

long been a byword, but Princess Marina would eye her daughter appraisingly and foresee the changes time would make.

As she grew up, Alexandra began to show promise of her mother's beauty. Bearing in mind the public role her daughter would soon be called upon to play, Marina wisely sent her to a finishing school in Paris. Always adaptable, Princess Alexandra entered with a will into her studies of French grammar, French and Russian literature, dressmaking and domestic science.

While the Princess was growing up, there was a shortage of royal ladies for the busy round of public engagements. George VI, who was particularly concerned that the monarchy should have as much good publicity as possible, recognized in his niece a charm and natural manner that would be welcome in public life. As a result, Alexandra began to take part in royal duties while still much younger than most Princesses. She was only seventeen when she made her first public appearance at the presentation of prizes to the Junior Red Cross at St James's Palace in London. It was a daunting moment for a schoolgirl who had often been asked what it felt like to be a Princess and who had answered, 'The bother is that I often forget I am one.' She had to make the shortest of speeches, only thirty seconds long, but was quite stricken with terror. She said her words correctly and formally and then disarmed everyone by asking 'Was I awful?'

Sooner or later every member of the royal family must undertake rigorous tours as the Queen's representative overseas. It is a daunting prospect but Alexandra found it very stimulating, even down to the tiring effect of time and climate changes. By now she had slimmed down and developed a natural grace reminiscent of her mother's which the crowds who came to see her found very attractive. She went on tours to Thailand, Burma, Hong Kong and Japan. Even with her relatively small dress allowance she managed to shine—often literally—in brocades, silks and vivid colours as a form of tribute to the splendour of the countries she was visiting. She was a brilliant success in Australia and it was here that she began what is now quite common procedure on royal tours, stepping aside from the route to chat to someone in the crowd. On one memorable occasion on the Australian tour she stepped into an open car and sat down on her host's top hat. The country took this wholly natural royal lady to their hearts and christened her 'the dinkum princess'.

Always energetic, Alexandra found time to help at the Great Ormond Street Hospital for Sick Children.

Nursing has been something of a tradition in the Kent family and Alexandra sought no privileges or relaxation of the rules. She often stayed long after her colleagues had hurried off duty, to play with children, and no task was too unpleasant for her to deal with. She had always enjoyed looking after her baby brother Michael and seemed to have a way with children—oddly similar to the girl who was to become her sister-in-law, Katharine Worsley.

Alexandra first met Angus Ogilvy when she was still quite young, at the Beagles Hall at Eton College. They may even have met before but, as she herself said, 'hadn't noticed one another'. To his surprise, he

Alexandra always said that she would marry for love alone and she found her 'Prince Charming' in the shape of a tall, dark and handsome Scotsman.

had been asked to escort her to a party and was later congratulated on the way he had done it. She and Angus were invited to the same house parties and balls and began to see a lot of each other. Newspapers hinted at a possible romance. Meanwhile, Alexandra's elder brother's engagement to Katharine Worsley was officially announced. She was delighted, having known the 'inside story' from the beginning and being very fond of her future sister-in-law.

About this time, Princess Marina and her daughter moved from Coppins to Kensington Palace in London and Angus Ogilvy became a regular visitor. It soon became apparent to the family that the couple were very much in love and it was no surprise to them when Angus proposed and Alexandra accepted. The official announcement was made on 29 November 1962.

Although there had been rumours of romance, the

A delightful and informal glimpse behind the scenes as Princess Alexandra watches her husband give thank-you presents to the bridal attendants.

news came as something of a surprise. Everyone instantly wanted to know what the groom-to-be was like. He was, the newspapers said, tall, dark and handsome. He was a rich and successful businessman. Also, although he was simply the Honourable Angus Ogilvy, he came of an aristocratic Scottish family with royal connections. His grandmother had been lady-in-waiting to Alexandra's grandmother, Queen Mary, and his sister-in-law is an extra lady-in-waiting to the

present Queen. But much more important than his 'pedigree' was the fact that the engagement was obviously a love match. Years before, Alexandra had stoutly defended her right to marry for love and love alone, and the millions who later watched the wedding on television were struck by the obvious depth of the couple's feeling for one another.

The wedding took place on 24 April 1963 and the day dawned slightly chilly but with the 'sunny periods' which can make or break a day in the open in Britain. As on many royal occasions, the weather, in fact, made little impact on the thousands who lined the route to Westminster Abbey to cheer the bride. Of all the royal brides Westminster Abbey has seen, Alexandra seemed the least affected by nerves. As she walked that long distance to the high altar on the arm of her brother, the Duke of Kent, she seemed to be positively bubbling over with joy. Her dress glimmered under the glare of the television lights: the effect had been created by the designer, John Cavanagh, who had undersewn the gown with gold sequins. He had designed a simple dress, using fully seventy-five metres (eighty yards) of magnolia-tinted lace. The veil also formed the train, six and a half metres (twenty-one feet) long. It was an original and striking idea but it placed added strain on the tiara which secured it.

There were six child attendants, and twelve-year-old Princess Anne was the chief bridesmaid, looking very grown-up with her hair swept up and wearing a plain floor-length gown. She was the perfect organizer of the little ones, issuing whispered orders in French to the tiny and somewhat restless Archduchess Elisabeth of Austria, and making sure that they were all in the right place at the right time. As the beautiful processional music of 'Holy, Holy, Holy, Lord God Almighty' ended, the bride took up her place next to the groom, surrounded by representatives of many royal families, one of them the ill-fated Queen Victoria-Eugenie, one of Queen Victoria's granddaughters, who had been Queen of Spain. This joyous and very British occasion must have made her recall her own wedding so many years ago in Spain, when a terrorist bomb had killed about sixty people in the crowd, hurled the royal coach on its side and spattered the bride's dress and shoes with blood.

The television cameras stole glances at the assembled royal ladies: the Queen, grave in a pale green creation; Queen Elizabeth the Queen Mother in soft silver-grey; Princess Marina in a dramatic outfit of dazzling gold tissue; the young Duchess of Kent in a coolie-style hat of coral pink to match her coat and dress; and Princess Margaret looking remarkably happy in sunny yellow.

The bride made the traditional promise to obey and the responses of both bride and groom were proud and resonant. After the signing of the register, Alexandra made a deep curtsey to the Queen and Angus bowed. They left the Abbey to the wild cheers of the enormous crowd and drove to the wedding breakfast at St James's Palace.

This was a royal wedding with a striking innovation. For the first time, cameras were allowed behind the scenes. Although the usual formal photographs were taken, there were also some unique, informal pictures, characteristic of this 'people's Princess'. For example,

Princess Margaret was seen helping to arrange her cousin's train, Princess Marina settling the little Elisabeth of Austria and Princess Anne showing off her gold bracelet, given as a thank-you present to her as chief bridesmaid.

The first part of the honeymoon was spent at Birkhall, the Scottish home of Aunt Elizabeth, the Queen Mother (who had been delighted to loan it, too, to the young Duke and Duchess of Kent for part of their honeymoon). The newly-weds spent the rest of their honeymoon in Spain and then returned to live in Thatched House Lodge in Richmond Park on the Surrey border of London. This former royal hunting lodge and its beautiful garden provided a happy and secluded home for the young couple. There was one ugly incident there in the late 1960s when, despite all the security arrangements, a burglar broke in and managed to reach a room next to where the Princess was sleeping before he was caught. Alexandra was pregnant at the time and very distressed on her child's account.

James Robert Bruce Ogilvy was born on 29 February 1964, and his sister, Marina Victoria Alexandra, was born two years later. The Ogilvy family is a very private and happy one.

The decision to marry a Princess cannot be an easy one. One of the major contributory factors to the sad break-up of Princess Margaret's marriage to the Earl of Snowdon must surely have been their inability to resolve the tensions between their private life as man and wife and their public life as the Queen's sister and brother-in-law. Angus Ogilvy refused to accept a title and does not share in his wife's public duties, appearing with her only on those occasions when a husband would naturally be present. After an upheaval in the City, London's commercial centre, he resigned an important directorship and is now deeply involved in the work of several charitable organizations.

Princess Alexandra's special brand of charm and spontaneity keep her in constant public demand as a royal representative. She seems to grow more elegant day by day but she has never lost her approachability. She remains one of the most 'ordinary' royals, parking her car at a meter, buying her underwear at a well-known chain-store and actually carrying money—most unusual for a royal lady. When Alexandra was in her early twenties, the Queen bestowed the Order of Dame Grand Cross of the Royal Victorian Order on her, a regal sign of merit which she since has certainly earned several times over.

Princess Anne
&
Mark Phillips

Princess Anne was born at Clarence House in London on 15 August 1950, a little less than two years after her brother, Prince Charles. Brother and sister quickly became firm friends and are still very close now that they are grown up. The Queen and Prince Philip were determined to give their children as relaxed and normal a childhood as possible in their special circumstances. Certainly, Princess Anne's childhood was far less secluded and so much less intriguing to the public than that of her mother or aunt, Princess Margaret.

Lessons began at the age of five with Miss Peebles, who had been governess to the Duchess of Kent's children and who had made such a success of Princess Alexandra's early training. The policy of taking royal children out and about, begun by Queen Mary, was extended to include trips to museums, exhibitions and the zoo. When Prince Charles was sent away to preparatory school in 1957, the Princess missed her brother and constant companion and expressed a desire to be sent to school herself. The Duchess of Kent had broken new ground by sending her daughter, Princess Alexandra, to a school where she had been very happy. The Queen investigated the matter carefully and finally decided on Benenden, a boarding school in Kent.

In September 1963, the Queen accompanied her thirteen-year-old daughter to school. The Princess has a naturally sociable nature and quickly adapted to her new way of life. Like her mother, she values her privacy and enjoys occasional moments of solitude, so the busy communal life of Benenden must have seemed strange at first. She has never suffered from the shyness which seems to run in her family and she entered this new phase of her life with great enthusiasm.

The Princess has inherited her father's active interest in sport and her abiding love, like her mother's, is horse riding. The Queen taught her to ride on a Shetland pony when she was only three years old and she has never looked back. She began entering local gymkhana events on her pony, High Jinks, in 1962. In the school holidays she rode in the royal parks and during term-time High Jinks was stabled in Kent near Benenden for the Princess's weekly riding lessons. In 1968, she began entering serious competitions on her first horse, Purple Star.

Important though her riding was to her, the Princess

Previous page The wedding in Westminster Abbey was a glittering state occasion. The Princess became plain Mrs Mark Phillips but the happy bride was as pretty as a picture.

was also a young woman in the exciting 1960s and, naturally, enjoyed the company of young men. For some time the young Earl of Caithness was her favourite boyfriend and she kept his photograph on her bedside table. Later, the photograph was replaced by one of Guy Nevill, son of Lord and Lady Rupert Nevill, close friends of her mother. The Princess enjoyed going out and about and meeting many different people.

In 1968, she left school and began to show great interest in fashions. She developed a style of her own, not without causing considerable comment in newspapers and women's magazines, with her short skirts and peaked hats. She began, too, to lead an active and busy public life, still sparing as much time as possible for show-jumping and eventing.

It was, perhaps, inevitable that when she fell in love, it would be with someone who shared her passionate interest in show-jumping and who would be her equal in skill as a rider, if not in status. For some time the Princess's name was linked with various names from the equestrian world, including the dashing and handsome Richard Meade. But there were relatively few young men who fitted these somewhat exacting requirements and it was, perhaps, predictable that she should finally marry Lieutenant Mark Phillips, whom she met when she competed against him in the show-jumping arena.

To all who saw them together it became apparent that the young Princess and the Lieutenant were deeply interested in each other. They were constantly pursued by reporters and photographers from British and foreign magazines and newspapers. A denial of any romance was issued from the Palace but the press and public remained unconvinced. A second denial after the Princess had said a fond farewell to Mark at the port of Harwich as he left to rejoin the Queen's Dragoon Guards in Germany was equally ineffective in silencing speculation. On 29 May 1973, the rumours and guesses were finally silenced by an announcement from the Palace:

'It is with the greatest of pleasure that the Queen and the Duke of Edinburgh announce the betrothal of their beloved daughter the Princess Anne to Lieutenant Mark Phillips, the Queen's Dragoon Guards, son of Mr and Mrs Peter Phillips.'

Mark's family was invited to Buckingham Palace

Anne and Mark

No pre-wedding nerves but a lot of joy for this thoroughly modern Princess as she relaxes in typically casual style with her fiancé, Mark Phillips, in the elegant grounds of Frogmore House, Windsor.

for a celebratory family lunch. Photographs taken in the garden afterwards show a group of happy, relaxed parents delightedly discussing future plans. Now the secret was out, it seemed that the engaged couple were made for each other. The cheers that greeted the Princess on her public engagements had an added warmth. When the happy couple appeared together at horse shows, the applause was overwhelming and it was not just for their skills as riders. All the world loves a lover and a royal romance has a magical attraction like no other.

Mark Phillips was already used to the interest of the sporting public, and when he was plunged into the

wider public gaze, remarked to the press,

'Every day people pick up the paper and read about some disaster . . . I think they are rather relieved to read about something that is genuinely happy and good.'

If one source of speculation had been ended, there was all the excitement of the wedding plans to fill the gap. The Princess herself wanted the wedding to be a family affair and, in any case, it did not fall into the official category of 'an occasion for national rejoicing'. It would not be a State occasion, a title reserved, according to protocol, for events decreed to be of national importance or directly concerned with the Queen herself, such as her coronation or silver

of State of the Commonwealth countries had been informed. Also protocol dictated that the wedding take place within six months of the announcement. The date chosen was 14 November which, by a happy coincidence, was Prince Charles's twenty-fifth birthday and, almost to the day, the twenty-sixth anniversary of the Queen's wedding. Like her mother, the Princess was to be married in Westminster Abbey.

Following the tradition of twentieth-century royal brides, the Princess, escorted by her father, would travel to the Abbey in fairy-tale style in the Glass Coach, drawn by magnificent grey horses from the Royal Mews. The coach was originally bought by King George V and used at his coronation. The Queen's own parents had used it at their wedding in 1923, and so had the Queen herself, Princess Margaret and Princess Alexandra when they were married. Now it was despatched to the royal coach painters in Edinburgh to be made ready for the great occasion. The maroon paintwork on the doors, the gilded crowns on each corner of the roof and the blue silk upholstery were all refurbished.

Captain Eric Grounds, aged twenty-five and a brother officer of the bridegroom's, was chosen to be best man. Princess Anne chose her nine-year-old brother, Edward, and their cousin, Lady Sarah Armstrong-Jones, also nine, as her bridal attendants. Wishing to keep the wedding as simple as possible, the Princess opted for just two attendants instead of the eight bridesmaids and two pages who had been in her mother's bridal procession. She had been a bridesmaid herself and her desire to dispense with 'yards of unmanageable children' may have sprung from her experience of Princess Alexandra's wedding where, as chief attendant, she had been responsible for the six little bridesmaids, including the irrepressible Archduchess Elisabeth of Austria.

Not only was the bride Colonel-in-Chief of various regiments in her own right, but she was about to become an army wife. There was no doubt in her mind that the Army Catering Corps should have the honour of making the wedding cake. Meanwhile, the wedding ring was being fashioned from a nugget of gold mined

wedding. Whatever the official point of view might be, it was obvious from the enthusiasm which greeted the news of the engagement, that the nation intended to rejoice with the Princess and her family.

State occasion or not, the only daughter of the first family in the land could not hope to escape all the demands of protocol. Before the engagement was announced publicly, the Prime Minister and the Heads

A shared passion for show-jumping and equally great equestrian skills are the recipe for a happy marriage, if Mark's and Anne's smiles are to be believed.

in Wales, which had already provided wedding rings for the Queen Mother, the Queen and Princess Margaret. Newspapers speculated about the bride's bouquet. The Queen Mother and both her daughters had carried white orchids, a gift of the Worshipful Company of Gardners. Would the Princess follow suit? No one would know until the day, but it was certain that the bouquet would include the traditional sprig of myrtle, picked from the bush growing at Osborne.

The most intriguing question of all was the matter of the wedding dress. When the Princess first began to establish a fashion style of her own, one designer, Maureen Baker of Susan Small, had provided many of her outfits. Much to her astonishment, Mrs Baker was asked to put forward suggestions for the wedding dress and she and the Princess talked over the various ideas. Even by the beginning of October, no final decision on the style had been taken but perhaps this was wise because it made the likelihood of 'industrial espionage' far less. Like most brides, the Princess wanted the dress to remain a secret until the great day.

The bridegroom and best man did not have any problems about how they should dress. The wedding was to have a strong, military flavour out of deference to the bridegroom's profession. They would wear the full dress uniform of their regiment, the Queen's Dragoon Guards. The regiment would provide the Guard of Honour to line the Abbey entrance and soldiers would hand out the Order of Service inside the church.

The young couple drew up a guest list and at the beginning of October, 1,500 invitations to the ceremony were sent out. Only Heads of State who were also relatives or friends were included. The emphasis was on close friends of both families, high-born or not. Prince Rainier and Princess Grace of Monaco attended, so did Crown Princess Beatrix and Prince Claus of the Netherlands, King Constantine and Queen Anne-Marie of Greece, and there was a place for friends from the horse-riding world which had played such a part in their romance, including Alison Oliver and Richard Meade. Staff from the royal household and from the Phillips's comparatively modest country establishment were also included.

However much the Princess wanted the wedding to be a family affair, this was an event the whole world wished to attend. The British Broadcasting Corporation was inundated with requests from abroad for live coverage of the wedding via satellite. The BBC planned eight hours of broadcasting and this was the first royal wedding to be televised in colour and broadcast in stereo. In deference to the family's wishes, there were to be no pictures of the couple as they took their vows, or of members of the family during the service, or of the Queen as she said goodbye to her daughter for the last time as a single girl in the courtyard of the Palace. Some moments, it was decided, are too private for the eye of the camera.

As the date drew nearer, wedding gifts by the thousand flooded in from all over the world and they were put on display in St. James's Palace in London. Anne and Mark went to listen to the proposed hymns and organ music in order to make their final choice. Mark caused his own minor controversy by insisting on the inclusion of his regimental march, a brisk work by Johann Strauss, more suited to the trotting horses

which it usually accompanied than a dignified exit from church. The official wedding programme went on sale. Instead of having the usual monogram and coat of arms on the cover, it departed from precedent and showed a photograph of the happy smiling couple.

On the evening of 12 November, the Queen and the Duke of Edinburgh entertained over one hundred guests to dinner in the Throne Room at Buckingham Palace. Later, they were joined by nearly fourteen hundred wedding guests at a pre-wedding reception in the State Apartments. All eyes were, of course, on the couple at the centre of events, Anne and Mark.

The wedding day of the Queen's daughter and her handsome dragoon, 14 November 1973, began with pale wintry sunshine. The chill air did not deter the crowds who had been gathering since early morning along the route and round the Palace and the Abbey. The horses, groomed to perfection, were harnessed to the coaches. Troops lined the processional route and the Palace balcony, draped in scarlet and gold, made a splash of colour against the stonework. As the fifteen hundred guests assembled, the first coach of the carriage procession, carrying members of the royal family, emerged from the Palace, the clatter of hooves almost drowned by the cheers of the crowd. Inside the Abbey, the bridegroom's parents and other close members of his family took their places on the left rather than the right of the altar, because this was a royal wedding.

Just before eleven o'clock the Queen said goodbye to her daughter and took her place in the Scottish State Coach with the Queen Mother, the Prince of Wales and Prince Andrew. A Sovereign's Escort of Household Cavalry took up its position as the coach drew out of the Palace and all eyes were on the mother of the bride, a striking figure in sapphire blue. As the Queen entered the Abbey, a fanfare of trumpets sounded and reporters searched her face for signs of motherly emotion. Certainly there was an air of excitement about the Queen which had not been noticeable at other royal weddings she had attended.

Twelve minutes after the Queen's departure from the Palace came the moment everyone was waiting for —the first glimpse of the bride, sitting serenely by her father in the fairy-tale Glass Coach. The Princess was a breathtaking figure, totally captivating in a gown of pure white silk, high-necked and full-sleeved. The diaphanous silk veil, specially woven by a Suffolk firm, was held in place by a diamond tiara lent by the Queen Mother. Princess Anne, fourth in line of succession to the throne and second lady in the land, was truly a radiant bride as she made the short journey to the Abbey to marry the man she loved. Beside her, the Duke of Edinburgh, resplendent in the full dress uniform of a Field-Marshal, looked every inch a proud father as he acknowledged the crowd's cheers.

As the Princess reached the altar, Mark turned slightly and gave her a reassuring smile. The Archbishop of Canterbury, assisted by the Dean of Westminster, began the ceremony. The solemn words spoken were the same as in any church wedding in the land, however magnificent the setting, pomp and pageantry, as the Princess and Mark were married. Anne had already announced that she would follow tradition and promise to obey her husband. Supporters of women's liberation were duly appalled and realists wondered at this sudden submissiveness on the part of the strong-willed Princess.

After the vows were uttered and the Archbishop had given the newly-weds the solemn blessing, the young couple and their families moved into the Chapel of St Edward the Confessor to sign the register. After this, Mark and Anne were man and wife. Before leaving the Abbey, they paid homage to the Queen: they paused before her and their curtsey and bow set the seal of solemnity on the occasion, reminding the millions watching that the Queen is, indeed, Head of Church and State, as well as of her own family.

As the new Mr and Mrs Phillips left the Abbey, the crowd went wild. There was no doubt that Anne looked stunning and Mark so very handsome in his uniform as they took their places in the Glass Coach which was to take them to their wedding breakfast at Buckingham Palace. That it was a family occasion was obvious when the television cameras zoomed in on the Queen, bubbling over with happiness and bobbing up and down excitedly as her daughter and new son-in-law left.

Crowds gathered outside the Palace and, according to custom, at precisely 1.35 p.m. the bride and groom stepped on to the balcony to acknowledge the roars of heartfelt good wishes from the thousands below. The rest of the family joined them and Prince Charles received a special cheer for his birthday. At four o'clock, the Palace gates opened and out came an open carriage, bearing the newly-weds, well-protected against the November cold. The Princess's going-away outfit was modern, simple and warm: trimmed with white mink collar and cuffs, the sapphire blue velvet coat exactly matched the central stone of her engagement ring. Mr and Mrs Phillips began their honeymoon at Princess Alexandra's home, Thatched House Lodge in Richmond Park. Before leaving for an idyllic holiday in the Caribbean, they watched a recording of their own wedding on television.

During the course of preparations for their wedding, news of Lieutenant Mark Phillips's promotion to the rank of Captain came through. There was widespread speculation about whether he would also be granted a title. Princess Margaret's husband, Antony Armstrong-Jones, was created Earl of Snowdon shortly after their marriage but Princess Alexandra's husband, Angus Ogilvy, had refused a title. At the moment the Queen's daughter remains plain Mrs Phillips, though, of course, still a Princess. Captain Phillips has given up his army career to take up farming and perhaps a title will be more appropriate if he later undertakes more public responsibilities.

Princess Anne's son, Peter, was seen by many as a special Jubilee present to the Queen and few photographs of Her Majesty are as joyous as those showing her visiting her daughter, son-in-law and first grandchild. Millions saw him display a marked lack of dignity during the television relay of the Queen's Christmas message that year when, gurgling happily, he tried to pull an extremely valuable brooch off his grandmother's dress.

Mark and Anne now live at Gatcombe Park, in Gloucestershire, close to the Princess's parents-in-law and to many of their riding friends. They spend their time farming, riding and playing with their young son. Marriage seems to have brought out Mark's self-confidence. When he was first in the public eye, his nerves made him seem a rather vague and unexciting personality. Now, however, things are very different. He is more assured, relaxed with journalists and also doing somewhat better than his wife in their chosen sport. Anne, who inherited her father's outspoken intolerance of presumption and intrusion into her family's privacy, has mellowed with marriage and motherhood and lost some of her abrasiveness. Following the example of her grandparents and parents, Princess Anne has found that, in their marriage, she and her husband complement, support, encourage and love each other.

Princess Anne's pride in her baby son, Peter, is matched by the Queen's joy in her first grandson. A Jubilee baby, Master Phillips already shows signs that he has inherited his mother's independent character.

Prince Richard of Gloucester
&
Birgitte van Deurs

Like Prince Michael of Kent, Prince Richard of Gloucester was one of the lesser-known royal faces, perhaps because of his natural diffidence and because he doesn't quite fit into the 'hunting, shooting and fishing' tradition of the male members of the family. Studious and well-educated, he has something of the look of the eternal student with a wayward lock of hair and glasses. He was born in 1944, the younger son of the Duke and Duchess of Gloucester and a first cousin to the Queen. It was always his older brother, William, who was the dashing one and whose activities were constantly reported in the newspapers—overland trips to the Congo, a diplomatic mission to Japan and numerous flying expeditions, among other exploits.

In the family tradition, Richard went to Eton College and then to Magdalene College in the University of Cambridge. He was popular with his fellow students who called him, affectionately, 'Proggie', from his initials *Prince Richard of Gloucester*. He led an active life as a student but, aware that too many student pranks might cast a poor light on the royal family, he was careful not to become too involved in the more high-spirited activities of his college. Unlike his second cousin, Prince Charles, his education was not a matter for committees of Church and State to worry over. Richard earned his university place easily and studied architecture from choice.

He was a twenty-two-year-old student when he was asked to tea by a lovely young lady of his acquaintance. She had asked a friend, Birgitte van Deurs, to act as her chaperone, a sensible precaution against rumours for those who entertain royalty. Birgitte, the daughter of a Danish lawyer, was just twenty and studying English at a language school. Although Prince Richard gallantly recalls his hostess in glowing terms, his attention on that occasion was very much on the pretty Danish student.

On the whole, royal romances tend to develop slowly because, as Prince Richard's elder brother said, you have to be certain about love and marriage if you're royal. Besides, the young Prince was about to embark on a career after he had graduated and Birgitte, too, intended to make her own way in the world. However, like any courting couple, Richard and Birgitte met regularly and frequently, going to the theatre and the cinema and having dinner together. If they went to dances together, the Prince took the name Richard Harrison to avoid publicity.

After he left university Richard joined a firm of architects in North London. Birgitte took a job in the commercial section of the Danish Embassy in the Knightsbridge district of London, for which she was paid £30 per week. As time went on, it became clear to them that they were truly in love and when they decided to marry, five years after meeting, they could hardly be accused of rushing. Prince Richard was at that time tenth in line of succession to the throne. Like all members of the royal family, he had to ask the Queen for official permission to marry. She was delighted to give her assent and the Privy Council formally approved the match on 4 February 1972. The official announcement of the engagement came from the Palace on 15 February.

Birgitte's father, Mr Asger Henrikson, was invited to the Palace for the formalities and a small celebration. Birgitte's parents were divorced and she had taken her mother's surname. News of any royal romance cheers people up and many wished the young couple well, although, because Richard was so little known, his engagement caused hardly a ripple of attention. The engagement photographs show a truly natural, almost 'ordinary' couple and the photographers were impressed by their 'niceness'.

The wedding was planned as a very modest affair with no more than ninety guests and just a slight sprinkling of royals. It took place on Saturday, 8 July 1972 at St Andrew's Church near the Gloucesters' family home, Barnwell, in Northamptonshire. The day started with rain but this failed to dampen anyone's spirit, least of all that of the chief guest, the Queen Mother, who carried her famous see-through umbrella with great aplomb from her car up to the picturesque country church. The other royal guests were Prince Charles, Princess Margaret and the Earl of Snowdon and the indefatigable Princess Alice of Athlone, in her late eighties and enjoying herself hugely. The Queen and Prince Philip were on holiday with Princess Anne, and the Duke and Duchess of Kent were attending the Wimbledon Tennis Tournament and so were unable to attend. Princess Alexandra had official duties during the day but was able to get to the reception. The best man was the groom's brother, Prince William, who kept consulting his watch nervously. The Duchess of Gloucester was

Right Richard and Birgitte invited only close friends and family guests to their quiet, country wedding.

Previous page Prince Richard married Birgitte, the daughter of a Danish lawyer, in July 1972. Less than two years later, they became Duke and Duchess of Gloucester.

present but, due to his poor health, the Duke was confined to the house and could only attend the reception.

The Dean of Windsor, assisted by the Bishop of Peterborough and the Vicar of Barnwell, conducted the service which included the family's favourite hymns, 'All Creatures of Our God and King' and 'Love Divine, All Loves Excelling'. It rained in earnest after the ceremony, so the newly-weds had to use a car to travel the short distance between the church and the house instead of taking the walk that they had planned. A small crowd cheered them and the 'quiet wedding' was over, except for the usual toasts and speeches.

They had planned a private life. To begin with, they were going to live in Richard's large flat overlooking the Regent Canal in London's Camden Town. Meanwhile, Richard's firm of architects were converting a warehouse beside the River Thames into a more luxurious home for them. Their idyllic plans went awry when, in August 1972, only a month after the wedding, Prince William, only thirty years old and heir to the dukedom, was killed in a flying accident. The whole royal family grieved—the Queen is said to have taken the news very badly. But after the funeral there was little time for private grief, for Prince Richard suddenly found himself the heir to a dukedom very close to the throne. The Duke of Gloucester was a younger brother of the late King George VI and Prince Richard now became ninth in line of succession to the throne.

This alteration in status meant an abrupt change in the plans of the Prince and his new wife. He began to undertake official engagements, both at home and abroad. There was little spare time and certainly not enough to maintain a career. Just over eighteen months after the untimely death of Prince William, the elderly Duke of Gloucester died and Richard now became the Duke of Gloucester and his very quiet, shy wife the Duchess. Gone was the promising career in architecture and gone was a very private life. Barnwell and Kensington Palace became their official residences: the flat in Camden Town and the home in a dockland warehouse went to others.

An additional strain on the young Duchess, so suddenly and unexpectedly thrust into the limelight, was her pregnancy. The baby, Alexander, was born two months premature in 1974 and had to be kept in an incubator. For a time he seemed worryingly frail

Their public roles were unexpected but Birgitte's charm and Richard's good humour soon made them welcome guests.

The Duke and Duchess are thrilled with their family, Alexander, Earl of Ulster, and Lady Davina.

but eventually he rallied and the young Earl of Ulster soon developed into a delightful and active toddler. His christening drew far larger crowds than the wedding of his parents two years earlier at the same church. Four thousand well-wishers were there and the much more confident Duchess delighted them by stopping from time to time to let them have a peep at her son.

In 1977 it was announced that the Duchess was among the three royal ladies expecting a 'Jubilee baby'. The family was anxious lest this pregnancy, too, would not be trouble-free, but, happily, a daughter, Davina, entered the world during the Queen's Silver Jubilee celebrations.

The Duke and Duchess of Gloucester, thrust so sharply into public life, have grown in style and confidence. The Duchess, particularly, appears to have a very royal self-composure and always looks very elegant; the Duke, happiest when talking to fellow architects or discussing town planning, has grown skilfully into his role as one of the Queen's helpers.

Prince Michael of Kent
&
Marie-Christine von Reibnitz

Of all the Kent family, Prince Michael has been the least known. As his elder brother, Eddie, the Duke of Kent, grew up he came to resemble his father, not just in looks but in character. As the Queen's first cousin, the Duke of Kent has undertaken a share of the royal responsibilities and his warmth and charm ensure his welcome at public functions. Princess Alexandra, too, is a well-known and much-loved figure at home and abroad and has frequently represented the Queen in her own special and relaxed way. But Michael has never been in the public eye very much and tries to avoid contact with the press.

Above *The newly-engaged couple little realized the problems soon to beset their wedding plans.*

Previous page *Prince Michael's wedding to the divorced Marie-Christine was dogged by doctrinal difficulties.*

However, when his controversial engagement to the Austrian Baroness Marie-Christine von Reibnitz was announced at the end of May 1978, it was no longer possible to avoid publicity.

Marie-Christine, two years younger than Michael, is a Roman Catholic. She was educated in a convent and became a successful interior designer in London. In 1971, she married Thomas Troubridge, a merchant banker, but the marriage was not successful and the couple separated. After two-and-a-half years, in August 1977, they were divorced by mutual consent. Marie-Christine, a devout Catholic, knew that her Church would not recognize her divorce and applied for an annulment of her marriage. For this to be granted, evidence must be produced to show that there was a serious obstacle to a valid contract at the time of the wedding. A number of different things may constitute an obstacle, such as a lack of intention to remain faithful or a refusal to have children. The proceedings take place in secret and there were three separate hearings for Marie-Christine's case. Finally, an annulment was granted in May 1978. In her own eyes and those of her Church, Marie-Christine was a single woman and free to marry.

However, this was by no means the end of the problems. The Act of Succession of 1700, forbids members of the British royal family to marry Roman Catholics. In order to marry Marie-Christine, Michael had to renounce his right of succession to the throne. He was quite willing to do this on his own behalf and, for all practical purposes, it made little difference to his position, because many senior members of the royal family precede him in order of succession. However, he was not prepared to renounce the right on behalf of his descendants. This was not an insurmountable problem: it simply meant that any children of the marriage between Michael and Marie-Christine must be raised as Anglicans. As the couple very much wanted a family, they considered carefully and agreed to such an arrangement.

In May 1978, Michael requested the Queen's permission to marry Marie-Christine. She consented without making any conditions or commenting on the religion or status of any future children. It seemed as if all the major difficulties had been overcome and the couple began to plan their wedding. They could not be married in England or Wales: the Church of England opposes the remarriage of divorced people in church. The couple could not marry in a register office either, as the royal family was specifically exempted from the 1949 Marriage Act, covering register-office weddings,

because at that time it was thought that none of them would ever want a civil wedding. They could not marry in a Roman Catholic Church, because it would be illegal for a registrar to perform the civil side of the marriage. They could have chosen to be married in Scotland, where the law is different, but they finally decided on the Schottenkirche in Vienna, where the bride's grandmother and great-grandmother had been married. Afterwards, the marriage could be registered with the British Consul under a reciprocal arrangement. The wedding was planned for July and they intended to invite both the Duke of Kent and Princess Alexandra to the ceremony and to include members of both families among the bridesmaids.

It seemed as if their future together was now certain. Michael would continue to be a member of the Church of England and would raise his family to be members of it, too. Marie-Christine would con-

Neither the disappointments and difficulties nor the public debates which preceded the wedding could spoil the intense happiness of the bride and groom.

tinue in the Catholic faith and her marriage to the man she loved would be recognized by her Church. There was only one more matter to settle. As a rule, the Catholic Church raises no difficulties about 'mixed' marriages, but it does expect children of the marriage to be brought up as Catholics. If there are special reasons—as there were for Michael and Marie-Christine—for bringing up the children outside the Catholic faith, Papal dispensation is necessary. As soon as the Queen's permission had been granted, the couple petitioned the Holy See for this dispensation. It is not automatically granted but they were very optimistic. They hoped that their marriage would be a 'positive demonstration' of the new ecumenical spirit in religious circles.

The plans for a white wedding were well advanced when it was announced in June that the Pope had refused to grant the dispensation. This was a shattering blow and the couple were very distressed. They had to made a sudden change in their plans and arranged for a civil wedding in Austria on 30 June. Marie-Christine was particularly unhappy as a civil marriage would not be recognized by the Roman Catholic Church and this would cause problems in the practice of her religion. For example, she would be expected to abstain from receiving communion, an act central to her faith.

Newspapers had followed the story of the 'star-crossed' lovers with interest and now there was a blaze of publicity. Everyone seemed to have something to say on the subject and feelings ran high. The Church of England leaves the religion of children to be decided jointly by their parents and has often criticized the Roman Catholic attitude to 'mixed' marriages. Although there was no question of a formal protest, as Prince Michael was going against Anglican teaching by marrying a divorcée, clergymen were outspoken in their disapproval of the Pope's decision. On the other hand, many Catholics believed that dispensation was rightly refused. There were rumours that the rules for annulment had been relaxed just because it involved a member of the royal family. The Pope's refusal was seen as proof that this was not true, although, in fact, there had never been any evidence that it was.

Letters poured into the newspapers and public statements were made. The fundamental question was difficult to understand and many seemed to expect either the Roman Catholic Church or the Church of England to reverse centuries of teaching more or less overnight. Even Prince Charles rather rashly joined in the debate. At the opening of the Salvation Army's international congress in London, he criticized church authorities and the arguments about doctrinal matters, 'which can only bring needless distress to a number of people'. His uninformed comments caused a great deal of anger in the Roman Catholic community and among clergy.

Amidst the furore, Michael and Marie-Christine went ahead with their wedding on the last day of June. A brief civil ceremony took place in Vienna's neo-Gothic town hall. About twenty close relatives attended, including the Duke of Kent, Princess Alexandra, Angus Ogilvy, Princess Anne, Lord Mountbatten and Lady Helen Windsor. No one officially represented the Queen. Michael forgot to take his passport to the ceremony and had to send

an official to the British Embassy to fetch it. Otherwise, there were no hitches and in the evening a sparkling assembly of guests attended a dinner at the seventeenth-century Schwarzenberg Palace Hotel. The couple spent the first night of their married life apart as the bride wanted to attend a private Mass the following morning. She felt it would set a calm and

religious seal on their marriage.

After all the obstacles and difficulties, Michael and Marie-Christine have found real happiness and fulfilment together. They live a very quiet and private life, now that all the fuss surrounding their wedding has died down and the fierce spotlight of publicity has been turned off.

The Queen welcomed the new member of the royal family by attending his christening at the Royal Chapel, St James' Palace in July 1979.

In 1979, their first son was born and family life is proving to be the joy they hoped for and deserve, after the stresses of their courtship.

Charles,
Prince of Wales

The birth of Prince Charles Philip Arthur George, the first child of Princess Elizabeth and the Duke of Edinburgh, on 14 November 1948, thrilled his proud parents and the entire nation. By the time his mother became Queen and he became the Heir Apparent, in February 1952, Charles had a younger sister. Separated by only two years' difference in age, he and Anne quickly became firm friends and have remained very close ever since.

The Queen's own family life had been especially happy and she was determined to create the same loving and warm atmosphere for her children. She recalled how very frequently in childhood she had appeared in public and made up her mind that her own children should lead much more private and 'normal' lives. She also undoubtedly remembered her parents' policy of making little distinction between their two children and she decided on the same approach for Charles and Anne. In many ways this was a sensible decision and avoided unnecessary rivalry and jealousy, but it did mean that the little boy tended to remain babyish longer than his contemporaries. Identical clothes for the little Princesses Elizabeth and Margaret Rose were both acceptable and charming, but Charles's button shoes and coats with little velvet collars made him appear girlish and silly at times.

The Duke, too, was anxious to give his family a secure and stable background. His own parents had separated when he was still quite young and this made him particularly determined to be a father in the fullest possible way. But his childhood had also been a period of immense freedom and he was firmly convinced that a similar way of life would be right for Charles. He had attended a preparatory school and then Gordonstoun in Scotland and believed that the self-confidence, self-reliance and toughness taught there were valuable attributes for a future King.

To begin with, the royal children's education was supervised by their governess, Miss Peebles. In January 1957, Charles went to his first school, Hill House, in Knightsbridge in London. It was the first time the heir to the throne had actually attended a school, rather than receiving his education at the hands of tutors. The following autumn, he went to his first boarding school, Cheam, which his father had attended. The headmaster had been asked not to give the Prince any preferential treatment and two or three times he was punished for his misdeeds with a spanking. This was by no means a novel experience for Charles, as the Duke is a firm disciplinarian and expected obedience from his children.

Charles was quite lonely when he was first away from home and the familiar companionship of his sister. Having inherited the Queen's shyness, he didn't find it easy to make friends, and other boys were hesitant about making friends with him.

During his time at boarding school, the Queen bestowed the title of Prince of Wales on him. On 26 July 1958, a pre-recorded message from the Queen was broadcast at the closing of the British Empire and Commonwealth Games in Cardiff (the Welsh capital), which she had been unable to attend. She said,

'The British Empire and Commonwealth Games in the capital, together with all the activities of the Festival of Wales, have made this a memorable year for the Principality. I have, therefore, decided to mark it further by an act which will, I hope, give as much pleasure to all Welshmen as it does to me. I intend to create my son Charles, Prince of Wales, today. When he is grown up I will present him to you at Caernarvon.'

In 1962, when Charles was thirteen, the Queen and Prince Philip, continuing their policy of an all-round education for their son, decided to send him to his father's old school, Gordonstoun. Naturally extrovert and physically active, Prince Philip had delighted in the tough regime, but many people doubted its suitability for his sensitive, gentle and more artistic son. The boys came from all kinds of backgrounds but were treated alike. Charles had to get used to early morning runs, cold baths, period of intensive study, frugal meals and the open air life. However, he *did* get used to them and looks back on the days he spent at Gordonstoun with real affection. Once again, he found making friends something of a problem to begin with, but, after a term, he gathered a group of personal friends round him and many of them have remained in close contact with him.

At Gordonstoun, Charles soon proved himself to be a very good 'all-rounder' academically. He worked hard and kept about middle of the class in most subjects. In 1964, he passed his 'O' Level General Certifi-

Right *Charles, a formal portrait. Created Prince of Wales in 1958, his investiture took place at Caernarvon 11 years later.*

Previous page *Lady Sarah Spencer, at one time a frequent companion, greets the polo playing Prince with a kiss and an affectionate hug.*

Prince Charles makes history in May 1962 as he greets his headmaster at Gordonstoun. Prince Philip, an old boy of the school, sees his son settle in.

cate of Education examination in five subjects. He developed his already active interest in sport and outdoor activities and played football, rugby and cricket, as well as running, fishing, swimming and sailing. During this time, too, he became deeply interested in music and learned to play the 'cello. He showed considerable talent and played with the Elgin Orchestra on one occasion. Another unexpected talent was revealed when he took the leading role in a school production of *Macbeth*. Gordonstoun gave the young Prince a new self-awareness and maturity, rooted firmly in the careful fostering of his own considerable abilities and character.

He began at this time to show his lively sense of humour and an ability to make witty quips 'off the cuff'. He became acquainted with the very British and idiosyncratic comedy of the popular 1950s radio series, 'The Goon Show'. Charles became a firm fan and accomplished imitator of the Goons' anarchic kind of humour. The Goons—Peter Sellers, Spike Milligan, Michael Bentine and Harry Secombe, all now famous entertainers on their own—became

highly valued friends. His ability to make others laugh and to take a joke against himself did much to ease him into the ordinary routine of daily life at Gordonstoun.

Inevitably, the press followed Charles's progress at school avidly and made it even more difficult for him to be an 'ordinary' schoolboy. Two incidents, which were blown up out of all proportion, caused him acute embarrassment. A national newspaper managed to obtain an exercise book containing a number of his essays. Some journalists even suggested that he had sold it himself because he was short of pocket money and, for some time, his housemaster was also under suspicion. From this tiresome episode Charles learned to consider his every move with extreme caution because, no matter how trivial an action seemed to him, it could, and often did, make headline news. Unfortunately, he didn't learn this lesson before the notorious 'cherry brandy affair'.

During a trip on the school yacht, Charles was waiting for a meal to be served at an hotel in Stornaway in Scotland. Feeling awkward about the number of people staring at him through the window, he escaped into the bar. He says,

'Having never been into a bar before the first thing I thought of doing was having a drink, of course. It seemed the most sensible thing. And being terrified, not knowing what to do, I said the first drink that came into my head, which happened to be cherry brandy, because I'd drunk it before when it was cold, out shooting. And hardly had I taken a sip when the whole world exploded round my ears.'

The press made a tremendous fuss about this episode and Charles was severely reprimanded by his headmaster and his parents.

He has often joked that it was as a result of the 'cherry brandy affair' that he was sent out of the country to Australia. In fact, Prince Philip decided that an exchange with a pupil from Geelong, the public school in Melbourne, would broaden his son's horizons, toughen him still more and keep him out of the public eye. The Queen welcomed the opportunity of allowing Charles to get to know well a country that was one of the most vigorous members of the Commonwealth. In February 1966, he flew to Australia, feeling very apprehensive about his reception, as he knew that Australians could be very critical and outspoken. He needn't have worried. His welcome

Prince Charles went to Trinity College a raw schoolboy but, between 1967 and 1970, he gained a new self-confidence and maturity as well as an Honours degree.

was warm and friendly and, by the time he left to come home, he had inspired lasting affection and respect. In turn, he had gained a deeper knowledge and understanding of Australia than any previous Prince of Wales and when asked how he had enjoyed his stay at Geelong, he replied,

> '*Absolutely adored it. I couldn't have enjoyed it more. The most wonderful experience I've ever had, I think.*'

It says much for the Prince's character that he did enjoy his Australian visit so much. Timbertop, Geelong School's annexe situated in the Australian Bush, was much tougher than Gordonstoun. The pupils ran cross-country twice a week in temperatures of about 30° Centigrade in the shade, played what Charles himself described as 'fairly fierce games', quite unlike organized football or rugby, made expeditions into the Bush every weekend, and had tree-chopping races.

He returned to Gordonstoun and, in 1967, was made Guardian of the School, the equivalent of head boy. He also passed the Advanced Level General Certificate of Education examination in two subjects, a creditable achievement.

In October 1967 he was enrolled at Trinity College, Cambridge, to study Archeology and Physical and Social Anthropology. He transferred to the Faculty of History the following year. He went to Cambridge, not for the dilettante university career of some of his ancestors, but as a serious student, intent on gaining a degree. He was studious rather than brilliant and his time at Cambridge was interrupted by his official duties and by a summer term spent at the University College of Wales in Aberystwyth. There, he studied Welsh history, language and current problems.

His investiture as Prince of Wales at Caernarvon Castle, promised by the Queen in 1958, took place in July 1969. It was a truly British and splendidly royal occasion, watched on television by millions all round the world. But, above all, it was a family occasion and the Queen's affectionate pride in her son was obvious to all. Charles was noticeably shy and clearly found parts of the ceremony something of an ordeal. Nevertheless, he made a short address in impeccable Welsh, an indication of his intention to be Prince of Wales in more than name. He has continued to take a special interest in the Principality, especially in the welfare of its young people.

After his time in Aberystwyth, Charles returned to the busy and exciting student life of Cambridge. Apart from working for his degree, he kept up his interest in music and took an active part in sport, doing particularly well at polo. But his greatest pleasure in his Cambridge days was taking part in two student revues. He had discovered how much he enjoyed being on stage when he was at Gordonstoun and his own particular brand of humour was in tune with the times. He was a leading light in both *Revolution* and *And Quiet Flows the Don*, entering wholeheartedly into many of the irreverent and extremely funny sketches and poking good-natured fun at himself. Pictures of the Prince of Wales sitting in a dustbin while he was interviewed, wearing a gas mask and flippers while delivering a spurious weather forecast, and 'fighting' a set of green bagpipes were splashed across the front pages of the national newspapers. Typical, perhaps, of his new-found self-confidence and his ability to laugh at himself was the one-line gag

when he strolled on to the stage and stood silent under an open umbrella. After a pause, he said, 'I lead a very sheltered life.'

In May 1970, Charles took his final examinations at Cambridge and obtained a second-class Honours degree. Though not a brilliant degree, it was a very

Above The world's most eligible bachelor and Davina Sheffield share a private joke as they have shared many private moments in their long-standing friendship.

Left During his years in the Navy, Charles proved to be tough, adventurous and a skilful helicopter pilot.

creditable one. Eighty-three other students, whose studies had not been interrupted in the same way as his, gained the same result. Lord Butler, the Master of Trinity College, said, 'The tutorial staff here are extremely pleased about it. This boy has come out with flying colours.'

Charles left Cambridge with more than a degree: he had a new ease of manner and an awareness of his own strengths and weaknesses. He had learned to overcome his shyness and to cope with the inevitable difficulties which the heir to the throne encounters in personal and public relationships. He had shared fully in student life and was more in touch with the realities

Vivacious brunette, Lady Jane Wellesley, has been a close friend of the Prince since childhood and is a Fleet Street 'favourite' for the future Queen.

of the everyday world than almost any other member of the royal family. People, especially young people, felt that they knew him and they liked what they knew.

Now a young man, Charles was set for a service career. In March 1971, he joined the Royal Air Force College at Cranwell in Lincolnshire. After an intensive training course, he was awarded his 'wings' as a pilot the following August. Prince Philip watched the graduation ceremony with obvious fatherly pride. It came as no surprise that, after this brief period with the RAF, Charles joined the Navy, following in the footsteps of his father, grandfather, great-grandfather and great uncle.

He entered the Royal Naval College, Dartmouth, in 1971 and served in the Navy for five years, relinquishing command of the mine-sweeper HMS *Bronnington* at the end of 1976. During these five years, he walked under the ice in the Arctic, became a highly-skilled helicopter pilot, went through arduous under-water training, undertook a number of exhausting and

sometimes dangerous courses and finally took command of his own ship. The *Bronnington* had always been a happy ship and remained so in the period under Charles's command. He learned to cope with the responsibilities of a ship's commander, the welfare of the crew, matters of discipline and morale. Respect is not easily won in the close-knit masculine world on board ship, where everyone's lives can depend on each man doing his job properly and promptly.

Since leaving the Navy, he has been increasingly busy about official duties. He applies himself with a good will to the 'office work' at Buckingham Palace and travels all over the world. Wherever he goes he is unfailingly courteous, deeply interested and always willing to 'have a go'—whether it is dancing a samba in Brazil or trying out a new surf rescue craft in Australia. He has a particular interest in education and feels a special responsibility to young people. In April 1977, he launched the Queen's Silver Jubilee Appeal, as its President, and in July of the same year, he was installed as Chancellor of the University of Wales. In January 1978, he succeeded his great-uncle, Earl Mountbatten of Burma, as President of the United World Colleges. He remains an active sportsman and whenever he has any free time he loves to swim, sail, ride and ski. His father was one of the best polo players in the country but Charles promises to outshine him.

As a child, Charles was unprepossessing with jutting-out ears and a weak chin, but as he has grown up, he has become increasingly handsome with a charming smile and a fine athletic build. He is beginning to bear a close resemblance to his great-uncle, Earl Mountbatten, who was generally acknowledged to be the best-looking man in the entire royal family. With his good looks, charm, polished manners, many abilities, wonderful sense of humour and, of course, his title, Charles is the most eligible bachelor in the world. He proved himself to be a man's man when he was in the Navy and is now showing himself to be as successful with the fair sex. He is immensely attractive to young women and he has an eye for a pretty girl. In an interview for a women's magazine, he said,

'I've fallen in love with all sorts of girls and I fully intend to go on doing so, but I've made sure that I haven't married the first person I've fallen in love with.'

Charles frankly admits that he enjoys the company of young women. He has been seen out and about with all kinds of girlfriends, although they are invariably good-looking, intelligent and self-reliant. He shows something of a preference for blondes and, understandably, likes his girlfriends to be discreet and somewhat 'publicity-shy'.

Charles most enjoys a quiet dinner for two. He appreciates good food and has a fine palate for wine. He also likes to take his girlfriends out in his car, which he tends to drive very fast. A romantic at heart, he will dance the night away at one of London's most exclusive night clubs, his arms round a beautiful girl and a contented smile on his face.

Charles's name has been linked with many girls. Some are long-standing friends and others have shared a brief, mild flirtation with him. Angela Nevill, an old family friend and one of Princess Margaret's bridesmaids, shares Charles's sense of humour and is a natural companion for him. The lovely, blonde Georgina Russel, with her gift for music, appealed to another side of Charles's character. They spent many pleasant evenings together, listening to records or playing music. Georgina is a proficient pianist, harpist and violinist and Charles still plays the 'cello. Lady Jane Wellesley, daughter of the Duke and Duchess of Wellington, was a childhood friend and their liking for one another developed anew when they had grown up: a shared love of music and art, and a great sense of fun, formed the firm basis for their friendship. Like all Charles's girlfriends, Lady Jane is very attractive—a brunette, not a blonde—and extremely lively and adventurous. She and Charles were seen together on numerous occasions and he went to stay on her father's estate in southern Spain. He also liked to visit her London home to spend a quiet evening with her. Speculation about a serious romance died down while Charles was in the Navy because his duties kept him away for prolonged periods. Since he retired from active service, he has again been seen escorting her on various occasions.

Charles has said that he would like to marry an English, or possibly Welsh, girl, but this clearly doesn't prevent him appreciating the charms of girls of other nationalities: when he met Laura Joe Watkins, the daughter of a high-ranking American naval officer, in San Diego he was immediately enchanted by her. Photographs of them dancing together reveal a strong mutual attraction. Laura Joe has since visited him in England.

Nevertheless, Charles does seem to prefer British beauties. Davina Sheffield, another blonde and full of fun, has been a close friend for many years. They have

Like any young man, Charles relishes the company of lively and attractive girls, but tongues wagged when he was seen with pretty, blonde Mrs Jane Ward.

been seen together in places as far apart as a quiet cove in Cornwall and a cattle station in Western Australia. Other names that have been linked with the royal bachelor include those of Lady Charlotte Manners, Caroline Longman, Lady Sarah Spencer, Lady Alexandra Hay, Lady Caroline Percy, Lucinda Buxton and divorcée Jane Ward. Quite a few of Charles's ex-girlfriends, including Lady Caroline Percy and Lady Sarah Spencer, are now engaged or married. 'Spot the future Queen' is a favourite Fleet Street game and rumours increase as the list of suitable ladies grows smaller. Lady Jane Wellesley and Davina Sheffield have both been at the top of the list of 'favourite' candidates for some time.

Charles is fully aware that the slightest hint of a romance will make headline news and that this puts an almost intolerable strain on his girlfriends and on his relationships with them. Some relationships have not been able to withstand the glare of publicity and a very few girlfriends have succumbed to the lure of telling their stories to the press. Other relationships have only existed in the fevered imaginations of journalists. A reported romance with Princess Caroline of Monaco had no foundation in fact and she is now happily married to French businessman, Philippe Junot. An Australian newspaper once featured a story of 'a secret romance with a married woman, 36', but the most spectacular piece of romantic fiction was published in 1977.

A newspaper announced that it was 'official' that Charles was to marry Princess Marie Astrid of Luxembourg. It claimed that an announcement from the Palace was imminent. Princess Marie Astrid is a Roman Catholic and Charles would be prevented by the Act of Succession of 1700 from marrying her and keeping his right to succeed to the throne, apart from the fact that, although the couple had met, there was no evidence of a romance. The perpetrators of the story were quite unworried by these two problems and confidently claimed that the Queen and Prince Philip had agreed to a 'novel constitutional arrangement': that any sons of the marriage would be raised as members of the Church of England and any daughters as Roman Catholics. There was no suggestion of what provision would be made in the event of no sons being born. Not only is such an arrangement unlikely: it would also be totally unconstitutional. Newspapers did report, however, that Buckingham Palace had denied that there was to be an engagement. But denials from the Palace have not carried much weight since rumours of Princess Anne's engagement to Mark Phillips were denied.

Prince Charles once made the mistake of saying publicly that he thought thirty would be about the right age for marriage. Since his thirtieth birthday, his girlfriends have endured even closer scrutiny than in the past. Naturally, the nation is interested in Charles's eventual choice of bride, not just because he is the Prince of Wales, but because he is one of the most popular members of the royal family. His warmth, sympathy, humour and good looks have inspired tremendous affection and his broad experience of the world, his courage and achievements have inspired respect. Ordinary people hope that this 'Prince of the people' will find the loyal and loving wife he deserves.

His own family is a very close-knit and happy one and Charles obviously cherishes the values and traditions of family life.

It is a belief he has put into words:

'I personally believe that the family unit is the most important aspect of our particular society.'

His parents' happy marriage is a fine example to him and he believes that marriage is a serious undertaking

Prince Charles, the elegant family man, with Lady Sarah Armstrong-Jones at Balmoral.

and a lifelong commitment, based on mutual love and understanding. He will make very sure before he asks a girl to become the Princess of Wales that she is the right girl.

Perhaps Charles has already made his choice. The royal family has always believed in the value of prolonged courtships to ensure that there will be room for doubts before marriage instead of regrets afterwards.

Whoever she is, as Princess of Wales and eventually Queen Consort, she will be undertaking an enormous responsibility but, undoubtedly, a handsome, loving, dutiful and talented husband will be more than sufficient compensation.

ALBERT, Prince Consort (1819–61). Second son of Ernest, Duke of Saxe-Coburg-Gotha. Full name: Francis Charles Augustus Albert Emmanuel. Married Queen Victoria, his first cousin, on 10 February 1840.

ALEXANDRA, Princess (b. 1936). Only daughter of Prince George, Duke of Kent. Full name: Alexandra Helen Elizabeth Olga Christabel. Married the Hon. Angus Ogilvy (b. 1928) on 24 April 1963. Children: James (b. 1964); Marina (b. 1966).

ALEXANDRA, Queen consort (1844–1925). Daughter of Prince Christian of Denmark, later King Christian IX. Full name: Alexandra Caroline Maria Charlotte Louise Julie, known to her family as Alicky. Married Edward, Prince Wales, later King Edward VII, on 10 March 1863.

ANNE, Princess (b. 1950). Only daughter of Queen Elizabeth II. Full name: Anne Elizabeth Alice Louise. Married Captain Mark Phillips (b. 1948) on 14 November 1973. Children: Peter (b. 1977).

ARMSTRONG-JONES, Antony—see Snowdon, Earl of.

BOWES-LYON. Family name of Queen Elizabeth, the Queen Mother.

CHARLES, Prince (b. 1948). Eldest son of Queen Elizabeth II. Full name: Charles Philip Arthur George. Created Prince of Wales in 1958.

CLARENCE, Prince Albert Victor, Duke of (1864–92). Eldest son of King Edward VII. Known to his family as Eddy. Engaged to Princess May of Teck, later Queen Mary, in December 1891.

EDWARD VII, King (1814–1910, reigned 1901–10). Eldest son of Queen Victoria. Full name: Albert Edward, known to his family as Bertie. Created Prince of Wales when one month old. Married Alexandra of Denmark on 10 March 1863. Children: Albert Victor, Duke of Clarence (b. 1864); George, Duke of York and later King George V (b. 1865);

Louise, Princess Royal (b. 1867); Victoria (b. 1868); Maud (b. 1869).

EDWARD VIII, King (1894–1972, reigned 20 January to 11 December 1936). Eldest son of King George V. Full name: Albert Edward Christian George Andrew Patrick David, known to his family as David. Invested as Prince of Wales in 1911. Abdicated 1936. Created Duke of Windsor 12 December 1936.

ELIZABETH, Queen consort (b. 1900). Formerly Lady Elizabeth Bowes-Lyon, daughter of the 14th Earl of Strathmore. Married Prince Albert, Duke of York, later King George VI, on 12 April 1923. Now known as the Queen Mother.

ELIZABETH II, Queen (b. 1926, reigned from 1952). Elder daughter of King George VI. Full name: Elizabeth Alexandra Mary. Married Lieutenant Philip Mountbatten, formerly Prince Philip of Greece, on 20 November 1947. Children: Charles, Prince of Wales (b. 1948); Anne (b. 1950); Andrew (b. 1960); Edward (b. 1964).

GEORGE V, King (1865–1936, reigned 1910–36). Second son of King Edward VII. Full name: George Frederick Ernest Albert. Known as Duke of York until he was created Prince of Wales in 1901. Became heir to the throne after his father on the death of his elder brother, the Duke of Clarence. Married Princess May of Teck, later Queen Mary, on 6 July 1893. Children: Edward, later King Edward VIII (b. 1894); Albert, later George VI (b. 1895); Mary, Princess Royal (b. 1897); Henry, later Duke of Gloucester (b. 1900); George, later Duke of Kent (b. 1902); John (1905–19).

GEORGE VI, King (1895–1952, reigned 1936–52). Second son of King George V. Full name: Albert Frederick Arthur George, known to his family as Bertie, the Duke of York until his accession. Married Lady Elizabeth Bowes-Lyon, later Queen Elizabeth, on 12 April 1923. Children: Elizabeth, later Elizabeth II (b. 1926); Margaret, later Countess of Snowdon (b. 1930).

GLOUCESTER, Prince Henry, Duke of (1900–74). Third son of King George V. Full name: Henry William Frederick Albert. Married Lady Alice Montague-Douglas Scott (b. 1901) in 1935. Children: William (1941–72); Richard, later Duke of Gloucester (b. 1944).

GLOUCESTER, Prince Richard, Duke of (b. 1944). Younger son of Prince Henry, Duke of Gloucester. Full name: Richard Alexander Walter George. Married Birgitte van Deurs on 8 July 1972. Children: Alexander, Earl of Ulster (b. 1974); Davina (b. 1977).

KENT, Prince Edward, Duke of (b. 1935). Elder son of Prince George, Duke of Kent. Full name: Edward George Nicholas Patrick. Married Katharine Worsley (b. 1933) in 1961. Children: George, Earl of St Andrews (b. 1962); Helen (b. 1964); Nicholas (b. 1970).

KENT, Prince George, Duke of (1902–42). Fourth son of King George V. Full name: George Edward Alexander Edmund. Married Princess Marina of Greece on 29 November 1934. Children: Edward, later Duke of Kent (b. 1935); Alexandra (b. 1936); Michael (b. 1942).

MARGARET, Princess, Countess of Snowdon (b. 1930). Younger daughter of King George VI. Known, when a child, by her full name, Margaret Rose. Married Antony Armstrong-Jones, later Earl of Snowdon, on 6 May 1960, divorced in 1978. Children: David, Viscount Linley (b. 1961); Sarah (b. 1964).

MARINA, Princess (1906–68). Daughter of Prince Nicolas of Greece. Married Prince George, Duke of Kent, on 29 November 1934.

MARY, Queen consort (1867–1953). Daughter of Francis, Duke of Teck, and Mary Adelaide, first cousin of Queen Victoria. Full name: Victoria Mary Augusta Louise Olga Pauline Claudine Agnes, known to her family as May. Engaged to Prince Albert Victor, Duke of Clarence in 1891. After his death she married his younger brother, the Duke of York, later King George V, on 6 July 1893.

MICHAEL, Prince (b. 1942). Younger son of Prince George, Duke of Kent. Full name: Michael George Charles Franklin. Married Baroness Marie-Christine von Reibnitz on 30 June 1978. Renounced all claims to succession on his own behalf on his marriage.

Children: Frederick (b. 1979).

MOUNTBATTEN, Lord Louis (1900–79). Younger son of Prince Louis of Battenberg and uncle to Prince Philip. Full name: Louis Francis Albert Victor Nicholas, known to his family as Dickie. Created Earl Mountbatten of Burma in 1947. Married the Hon. Edwina Ashley on 18 July 1922. Children: Patricia (b. 1924); Pamela (b. 1929).

PHILIP, Prince, Duke of Edinburgh (b. 1921). Only son of Prince Andrew of Greece and Princess Alice. Naturalized British in 1947, when he took the name Mountbatten. Married Queen Elizabeth II on 20 November 1947. Created Duke of Edinburgh in 1947 and a Prince of the United Kingdom in 1957.

SCHLESWIG-HOLSTEIN-SONDERBERG-GLUCKSBURG. The Danish royal house. Also the Greek royal house to which Prince Philip belonged before his naturalization.

SIMPSON, Wallis (b. 1896). Born Wallis Warfield in Baltimore, USA. Married (1st) Earl Winfield Spencer Jr in 1916, divorced 1927; (2nd) Ernest Simpson in 1928, divorced 1936; (3rd) HRH the Duke of Windsor, formerly King Edward VIII, on 3 June 1937. Became the Duchess of Windsor on her marriage but never accorded the titular dignity of HRH.

SNOWDON, Earl of (b. 1930). Antony Charles Robert, son of Ronald Owen Lloyd Armstrong-Jones. Married (1st) Princess Margaret on 6 May 1960, divorced 1978. Children: David, Viscount Linley (b. 1961); Sarah (b. 1964). Married (2nd) Lucy Lindsay-Hogg. Children: Frances (b. 1979).

VICTORIA, Queen (1819–1901, reigned 1837–1901). Only child of the Duke of Kent and niece to King William IV. Married Prince Albert of Saxe-Coburg-Gotha on 10 February 1840. Children: Victoria, Princess Royal (b. 1840); Albert Edward, later King Edward VII (b. 1841); Alice (b. 1843); Alfred (b. 1844); Helena (b. 1846); Louise (b. 1848); Arthur (b. 1850); Leopold (b. 1853); Beatrice (b. 1857). Through the marriages of her family, almost all the royal houses of Europe were related to the British royal family. She was the great-great-grandmother of both Queen Elizabeth II and Prince Philip.

WINDSOR, Duke of—see Edward VIII, King.

Index

Picture Credits

Camera Press 74,137,138,145,147,154/5.
Central Press Photos 27,33,36,40,44,55,58,67(L),77,
80,101,135,149.
Cooper-Bridgeman Library 50/1.
Reginald Davis 38,39,78,79,94,99,102,110,114,119,
126/7,150,151.
Sara Ellis 6.
Fox Photos 25,41,54,56,57,60,66,67(R),69,70/1,75,82,
83(L),89,91,100,109,118,122,131,132,148,
149.
Keystone Press Agency 29,31,34/5,37,61,62,65,85,
112/3,133,136,142/3.
The Mansell Collection 14,18,26,43.
Popperfoto 7,9,11,13,15,16,17,19,21,22,46,47,48,49,
52,59,87,92,95(R),97,98,103,105,152.
Press Association 107.
Rex Features 83(R),111,128,144.
Syndication International 4,76,95(L),115,116,120,
123,125,139,140,141,153.

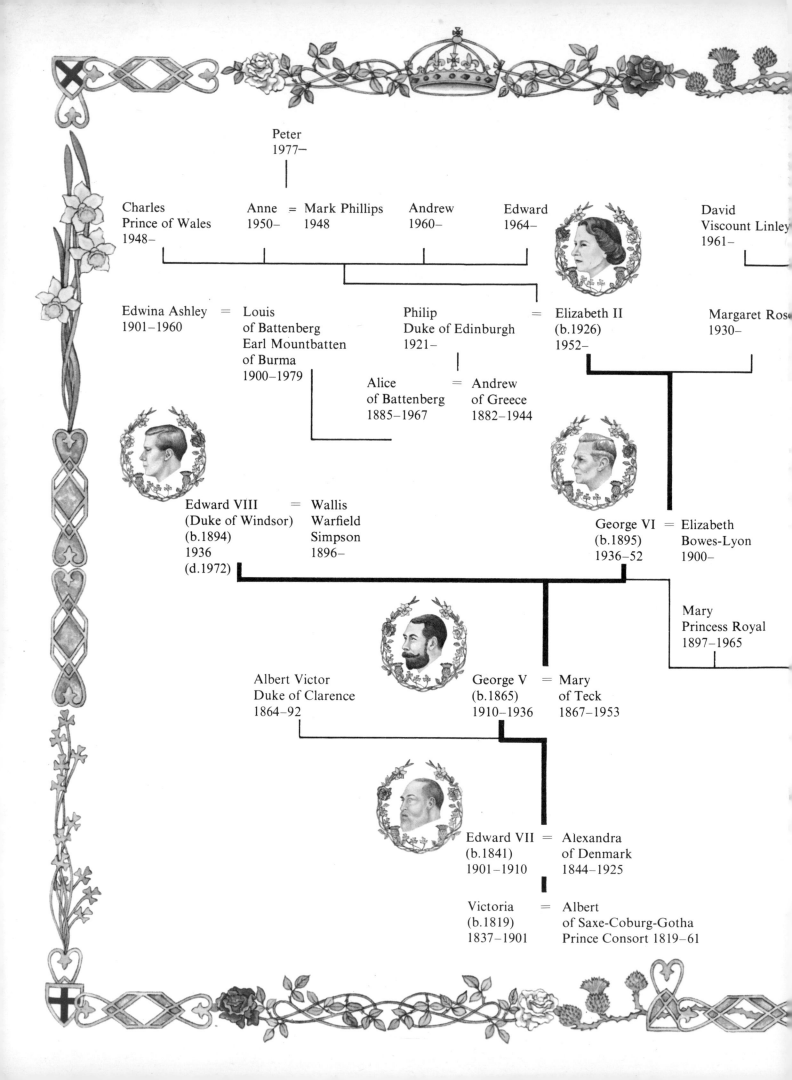

Peter
1977–

Charles
Prince of Wales
1948–

Anne = Mark Phillips
1950–   1948

Andrew
1960–

Edward
1964–

David
Viscount Linley
1961–

Edwina Ashley = Louis
1901–1960   of Battenberg
                Earl Mountbatten
                of Burma
                1900–1979

Philip
Duke of Edinburgh
1921–

= Elizabeth II
  (b.1926)
  1952–

Margaret Rose
1930–

Alice = Andrew
of Battenberg   of Greece
1885–1967   1882–1944

Edward VIII = Wallis
(Duke of Windsor)   Warfield
(b.1894)   Simpson
1936   1896–
(d.1972)

George VI = Elizabeth
(b.1895)   Bowes-Lyon
1936–52   1900–

Mary
Princess Royal
1897–1965

Albert Victor
Duke of Clarence
1864–92

George V = Mary
(b.1865)   of Teck
1910–1936   1867–1953

Edward VII = Alexandra
(b.1841)   of Denmark
1901–1910   1844–1925

Victoria = Albert
(b.1819)   of Saxe-Coburg-Gotha
1837–1901   Prince Consort 1819–61